The Sensitive Stance
in the Production of
Creative Ideas

The Sensitive Stance
in the Production of
Creative Ideas

Guy Aznar, Stéphane Ely

Editions Créa Université

Editions Créa Université

The Créa Université Association was created in 2006 by a group of Professors/Researchers in Creativity at Université Paris Descartes (France). Guy Aznar, Xavier Caroff, Sylvie Courcelle Labrousse, Stéphane Ely, Todd Lubart, Saphia Richou, Rémi Saint Péron, Olwen Wolfe, and Franck Zenasni currently serve on the board of directors.

The association's purpose is to conduct research programs and develop novel pedagogical tools, methods, and techniques for creative-thinking programs. The association offers a University Training Certificate in Creativity.

It is in the context of this research that we have written this book.

Editions Créa Université was created by the Créa Université Association, founded to encourage its members to publish their research, theoretical opinions, and clinical experiences.

The **Editions Créa Université** catalogue is available both digitally and in book form.

Guy Aznar and **Stéphane Ely**: "The Sensitive Stance In The Process Of Producing Creative Ideas." Editions Créa Université, Paris 2010 ©

© Editions Créa Université.
Contact@crea-univ.fr.   www.crea-univ.fr.
36 Boulevard de Sébastopol. 75004. Paris, France

Forward

Reinvent!

Man has always felt compelled to "reinvent the world." Perhaps this is so even more today because so much seems in need of being reinvented: our relationship to the Earth; how we define urban planning as more and more people migrate to cities; the way we eat, produce, move about, communicate; how we capitalize on economic ties and re-organize businesses to run more efficiently; how we prosper as human beings.

At the heart of our need to reinvent lies creativity, the core of collective life.

We are all creative beings. Ideas are always surfacing in our minds, both naturally and spontaneously. The question is how? Our aim is to understand the mechanisms behind the creation of ideas, to develop them, and then to teach and transmit that knowledge.

Depending on the person, group, or subject matter, are there various methods, techniques, and tools that can be applied to the process of creating ideas, thus helping to facilitate and amplify their production? Such is our question, as well as the object of our research.

This book investigates the fragile, often magical moment wherein ideas are born and emerge, exploring this interval equipped, as it were, with an imaginary diving suit and an intuitive-sensitive camera.

When we set about to invent, we call upon one of two thought processes: that of logic, kindred spirit of science, and that of creative thinking — two complementary paths that cross and that we use more or less unconsciously.

In the pages that follow we will explore creative thinking, and more particularly group creative thinking, which is our field of expertise. Creative thinking runs counter (temporarily) to that of logical thinking. There are two methods that can be used to suspend judgment (temporarily), break the chains of cause and effect, and disrupt the common neurological paths we take.
One strategy makes use of speed, firing off a series of thoughts and associations that bypass all judgment. This is commonly known as "brainstorming," but we will refer to it as the **dynamic stance**.

The other lesser-known strategy, and the strategy that especially interests us here, is in contrast slower-paced, seeking the vague quality of the intuition. We will refer to it as the **sensitive stance**. It assumes a more significant emotional input, as well as a more challenging group climate in order to bring the different imaginations together.

In both of these methods, creative thinking takes a "detour" from the straight line of logical reasoning. The "dynamic" detour is described by the terms "divergence" and "convergence."

The "sensitive" detour is described by the terms "departure," "emergence," and "sensitive convergence." These two strategies of the creative detour are compatible with and suitable to different subjects, personalities, and cultures.

In this book we will explore the sensitive stance…
- Because very little has been written about it.
- Because we feel that it opens up the imaginative field, giving rise to more forceful ideas that can then encourage potential rupture and/or an opening onto the future.
- Because we are partial to it.

In conclusion, we would like to stress that this creative-thinking method is but one ingredient in the global creative problem-solving process.

Because this book is inspired by our ongoing research on this subject, and in order to deepen our reflection, we would greatly appreciate your input.

Feel free to write us at www.creativite-sensible.com.

Guy Aznar   Stéphane Ely

                                           Paris, January 2011

THE SENSITIVE STANCE IN THE PRODUCTION OF CREATIVE IDEAS

Contents

Forward _____ 5

I. Invention: Two Thought Processes _____ 11
Logical Reasoning and Creative Thinking _____ 12
The Path of Logical Reasoning _____ 13
Creative Thinking: a Different Path _____ 15

II. Creative Thinking: Two Stances _____ 17
A Rapid, Quantitative Strategy: the Dynamic Stance, a Two-Stroke Engine _____ 22
- Brainstorming as Language _____ 23
- Brainstorming as Technique _____ 25
- Divergence and Convergence: the two creative Breaths of the Dynamic Stance _____ 27
- Stage 1: Divergence _____ 27
- Stage 2: Convergence _____ 27
- The Dynamic Stance: a Two-Stroke Engine _____ 30

A Slow-Paced, Fuzzy, Intuitive Strategy: the "Sensitive" Stance, a Three-Stroke Engine _____ 34
- "Little Bicycle": the Language of the Sensitive Stance _____ 35
- Stage 1: Departure – Toward the Imagination _____ 39
- Stage 2: Emergence of Ideas _____ 48
- Stage 3: "Sensitive" Convergence _____ 61
- Sensitive Stance: Emblematic Techniques _____ 62
- The Sensitive Stance, a Three-Stroke Engine _____ 62

III. Links between Creativity, Energy, and Emotion _____ 65
The Role of Energy in the Creative Process _____ 66
- Why does creative thinking expend such energy? _____ 66
- Origin of the Energy in the Creative Process _____ 67

Emotional Involvement in the Creative Process _____ 69
- How to Mobilize Emotion: the Group as Vehicle of Emotion _____ 69
- The Playful Emotional Engine of the Dynamic Stance _____ 70
- The More Intense, Authentic Emotional involvement of the Sensitive Stance _____ 70

IV. The Solution Finding Process _____ 72
The 3 meta-stages of the Solution-Finding Process _____ 75

The Standard Reference Process: Creative Problem Solving _____ 77

The Three Meta-Steps of the Solution-Finding Process from the Perspective of the Sensitive Stance _____ 79

Summary Table of Concepts linked to Creative Thinking Guy Aznar, Stéphane Ely _____ 81

In conclusion _____ 82

A New Look at Emergence _____ 82

Dynamic and Sensitive: Two Complementary Stances 83

A University Training Certificate in Creativity _____ 85

V. Annexes _____ 86

A Few Sensitive Techniques _____ 87

- Family 1: Departure Techniques for Imaginative Thinking _____ 88
  - Practical Guide: "Little Bicycle" _____ 89
  - Practical Guide: Identification _____ 94
  - Practical Guide: Analogy and Metaphor _____ 95
  - Practical Guide: Non-Verbal Departure Techniques _____ 96
  - Practical Guide: Projective Techniques _____ 100
- Family 2: Crossing-Over Techniques for the Emergence of Ideas _____ 104
  - Practical Guidelines: "Three Drawings" _____ 105
  - Practical Guidelines: "Pendulum" _____ 106
  - Practical Guidelines: "Orchestra Conductor" _____ 107
  - Practical Guidelines: "Staircase" _____ 108
  - Practical Guidelines: "Island in the Fog" _____ 108
- Family 3: Sensitive Convergence Techniques for the Elaboration of Ideas _____ 110
  - Practical Guidelines: "Hits & Highlights" - a dynamic convergence technique _____ 111
  - Practical Guidelines: Hits and highlights called "On the Fly" _____ 113
  - Practical Guidelines: intuitive clusters _____ 114
  - Practical Guidelines: sensitive development of clusters _____ 115
  - Practical Guidelines: "Concept Box©" _____ 115

Bibliography _____ 118

I. Invention: Two Thought Processes

Logical Reasoning and Creative Thinking

It is in man's nature to invent. Our human reasoning differentiates us from other animals, which are governed by instinct. Since the beginning of time, man has been driven to alter and transform the world — for its betterment or its detriment — and he has the neurological means by which to effect such change. He first created tools in order to dominate Nature (which might one day dominate him), performed the repetitive gestures required for their use, started to generate mental processes, and finally began to understand. Like the monkey Sultan whom Köhler studied, ancient man began by using a stick to retrieve a banana, inventing in the process a mental detour, then pulled the branch from the tree, and over time, by trial and error, began to invent increasingly complex processes.

There are two "thought processes" we can use when we undertake to invent something. One is logical reasoning, and the other we could call creative thinking, which situates itself outside the sphere of analytical thought.

The Path of Logical Reasoning

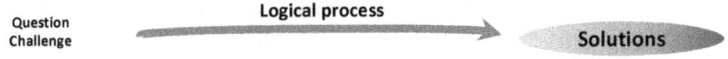

Question
Challenge — Logical process → Solutions

The process of logical reasoning proceeds by trial and error. We do an experiment with a stone, we try again with some fruit juice, and either it works or it doesn't. We record the outcome, then try again. We elaborate our theory (what if...?), and continue step by step, fitting the different experiments together like pieces of a puzzle: a piece either fits or it doesn't. The analytical process links cause to effect: the fundamental principle of rationality, as Kant explains in *Critique of Pure Reason*[1], where, in the attempt to make order out of chaos, we affirm that every effect has a cause, every phenomenon a rational explanation.

Linking words such as *and, therefore,* and *because* are used to connect our thoughts, much as nails, cogs of wheels, or notches of steel sheets are used to fasten, mesh, or connect things, creating a structure, such as a bridge to span the turbulent waters below.
In a forbidden forest, as in a child's bewildered brain, these words allow us to mark out trails.

After having taken the same neurological path over and over, from synapse to synapse, a network of paths imprints itself on the brain, much as footprints make marks in tender, wet grass, and this network is subsequently memorized.

---

[1] Emmanuel Kant, *Critic of Pure Reason*.

Over time man took logical reasoning to the heights of religious dogma. *"... never accept a thing as true until I know it as such without a single doubt,"* wrote Descartes[2]. As well as, *"Divide each difficulty into as many parts as feasible and necessary to resolve it,"* *"structure your thoughts beginning with the most simplistic,"* and *"imagine order even where it does not seem to exist."*

Logical reasoning has become what we now call scientific thought, as described by Claude Bernard in *An Introduction to the Study of Experimental Medicine*[3]: *"Enunciate the problem, come up with an hypothesis, carry out experiments, outline the results, interpret them, and present the conclusions."* The itinerary is well charted.

Logical reasoning is one of man's greatest achievements: the majority of our inventions can be explained by it, and most everything that surrounds us is beholden unto it: coffee machines and nuclear power plants, the rabies vaccination and digital books, the contraceptive pill and Google Earth, laptops and global warming. Rational thinking is what prevailed over obscurantism, superstition, and unfounded beliefs. Throughout history it has known its heroes and martyrs, like Giordano Bruno who was publically burned at the stake for his heroic writings and teachings that influenced progress in the development of medical cures, as well as the space missions of the twentieth century.

That being said, the potency of logical reasoning, its power and reassuring nature, have tended to obscure another reasoning process often quite opposed in its principles but complementary in its function.

---

[2] René Descartes, *Discourse on Method*.
[3] Claude Bernard, *An Introduction to the Study of Experimental Medicine*.

Creative Thinking: a Different Path

Inventive logical reasoning cohabits with another form of inventive thinking, but one that proceeds quite differently. It is called intuitive or creative thinking, and evokes Levi-Strauss's[4] "Savage Mind."

These two thinking processes are much like two itineraries by which one might travel though the same territory, or like two parallel planes in a non-Euclidean space that might brush up against each other from time to time, either colliding or connecting. Great inventions often come from such collisions of these mental planes.

Logical reasoning alone can produce inventions, following an "intuitive illumination." Creative thinking can likewise produce inventions. But more frequently, and in a manner both more beneficial and fertile, invention is a result of these two thinking processes working together.

The American psychologist J. P. Guilford demonstrated this fact in his theoretical studies and his experiments on intelligence. Human intelligence is not a unique factor (the "G" factor as it was called in the past); it is the result of a conjunction of factors[5]. He showed that at times logical reasoning is insufficient in resolving a problem; it needs a helping hand from a whole set of factors, including divergent thinking — or creativity.

---

[4] Claude Levi-Strauss, *Savage Mind*.
[5] Guilford spoke of 5-factors: cognition, memory, divergent thinking, convergent thinking, and evaluation (cited in *Psychologie de la Créativité* by Todd Lubart, Armand Collin, 2003).

It is precisely when he is bent over myriad test tubes or an interminable suite of equations seemingly leading nowhere that the savant begins to "switch off" his mind in order to invent.

As the anthropologist Levi-Strauss[6] wrote, *"... there are two distinct modes of scientific thought. They are certainly not a function of different stages of development of the human mind but rather of two strategic levels at which nature is accessible to scientific enquiry: one roughly adapted to that of perception and the imagination: the other at a remove from it. It is as if the necessary connections which are the object of all science, Neolithic or modern, could be arrived at by two different routes, one very close to, and the other more remote from, sensible intuition."*

"But it is important not to make the mistake of thinking," he continues further on, *"that these [scientific thought and mythical thought, which we compare to creative or intuitive thought] are two stages or phases in the evolution of knowledge. Both approaches are equally valid."*

---

[6] Claude Lévi-Strauss, *op. cit.*

II. Creative Thinking: Two Stances

Let us take a look at creative thinking for a moment in order to better grasp the contrasts.

Creative thinking does not follow a straight line or sequence of events as dictated by the law of causality. Instead, it takes a leap or a detour.

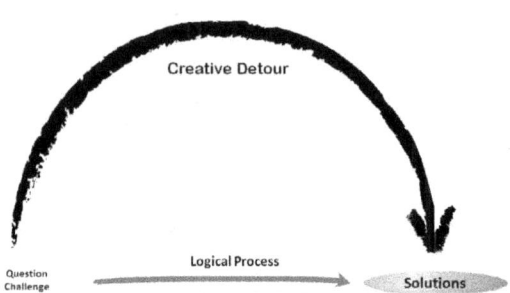

Like Christopher Columbus, who sailed off in search of the Indies, traveling in the wrong direction only to unintentionally discover an unknown continent, creative thinking is by nature rebellious.

Every description of the creative process speaks, in varying terms, of this "exiting the highway." Koestler[7], borrowing a notion from animal psychology, describes it as a detour. Guilford uses the word *divergence* . Souriau[8] expresses it as "thinking out of the box." De Bono[9] speaks of "lateral thinking." Anzieu[10] says we "take a step aside."

All of these metaphors speak to the fact that we leave the highways of thinking to adventure in unknown territory off to the side. In order to take a step aside, careless as it may be, we must avoid thinking too deeply; we must close our eyes and defer judgment, as Husserl advises in *On the Phenomenology*

---

[7] Arthur Koestler, *The Cry of Archimedes*.
[8] Paul Souriau, *Théorie de l'invention*, Hachette, 1881.
[9] Edward De Bono, *The Creative Problem Solver's Toolbox*.
[10] Didier Anzieu, *Le corps de l'œuvre*, Gallimard, 1981.

of the Consciousness of Internal Time[11], so as to experience the significance of things directly through our intuition. We regress to a childish form of thinking, returning to a primitive state of making drawings on walls. In so doing, we lose our bearings and abandon the fabulous parachute that the logical mechanism represents. We venture out, not knowing where we are going. Often frightened, feeling off balance, we travel in groups, holding each other's hands.

There are two strategies, or stances, we can employ to undertake this "sideways" voyage — both born of experience, then transmitted from generation to generation or garnered from books. The strategy that we call the dynamic stance utilizes rapidity, common sense, and game playing to short-circuit reasoning. The other strategy, which we call the sensitive stance, demands that we take a slow, deep plunge into the backwaters of the unconscious, following its spiraling movements until we bring to the surface pieces of raw ore that we then study with astonishment: the rough minerals of ideas we can then refine.

We will now give a brief description of these two strategies.

---

[11] Edmund Husserl, *On the Phenomenology of the Consciousness of Internal Time*.

THE SENSITIVE STANCE IN THE PRODUCTION OF CREATIVE IDEAS

A Rapid Quantitative
Strategy

GUY AZNAR. STEPHANE ELY. JANUARY 2011

The "Dynamic" Stance

A Rapid, Quantitative Strategy: the Dynamic Stance, a Two-Stroke Engine

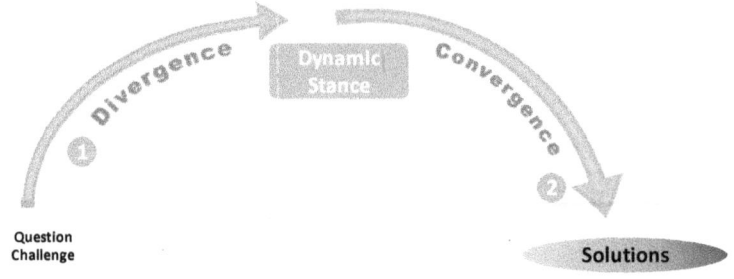

To move rapidly, impulsively, without taking the time to think or allow our minds to sort things out, without leaving room for daydreaming or going for a stroll, not giving in to the desire to run our fingers across the piano keys or drop a paintbrush haphazardly onto a piece of paper, this is the strategy used to subvert logical reasoning, leaving it no time to react.

In the world of ideas, this is the technique used in brainstorming. The expression *brainstorming* has become somewhat of a cliché, though historically it has had amazing success and is a term and method currently employed all over the world. Like the brand name Frigidaire, brainstorming has become a generic word. Whether in Beijing or Denver, Paris or Melbourne, when it seems that a discussion is going nowhere, whether it concerns a marketing campaign or a rugby tournament, at some point someone will raise his hand and say, "Why don't we brainstorm this problem?" In other words, let's stop thinking and say whatever comes into our heads, then we can sort through it all.

The term *brainstorming*, as coined by Alex Osborn, has become a brand name with both positive and negative aspects. On the positive side, it admittedly offers groups a new method of interaction. There is a "non-cogito ergo sum" dimension to its approach, which maintains that from time to time, and for a limited duration, each person in the group has the legitimate right to "suspend judgment" for the purpose of offering a new idea, putting forward a solution, as irrational as it may seem, which in an incontestable manner objectively favors the production of novel concepts.

On the negative side sits its extraordinary success. The globalization of the expression as a brand name has trivialized its meaning, turning it into a caricature of itself, something to be ridiculed, to the extent that today the word *brainstorming* is often used to designate anything and everything.

To talk sensibly about brainstorming, we believe it necessary to make a distinction between the two senses attributed to the word: that of language, as in **"brainstorming as language"** or associative language; and that of technique, as in **"brainstorming as technique,"** one different from other methods used to generate creative ideas.

Brainstorming as Language

Brainstorming as language uses a mechanism of associations: say whatever comes into your mind. Instead of connecting words, images, and concepts, respecting the structured laws of grammar and the logical principles of deduction and induction wherein each piece of information is connected to the one preceding it in what is called **objective causality** and which leads to an immediate understanding by all present (the word *kitchen* evokes the concept of food), words can be connected by the mechanism of what is called **subjective contiguity** (in my mind I associate the word *kitchen* with a white piano for reasons that I will not divulge). In free association, spontaneous expressions are connected through a relational system that is non-coherent, un-logical, random; they could also be a product of the geography of a person's unconscious, coming as it were from behind one's back.

The rules of free association are not specific to brainstorming; the same rules are applied in psychoanalysis. When someone lies down on a psychoanalyst's couch for the first time, he is instructed to say whatever comes into his mind, to free associate without criticism or judgment, even if what comes out seems silly. We could just as well say that the patient is lying there brainstorming since the rules are the same.

Likewise, in a Rorschach test, a person is asked to describe what he sees in the inkblots, to say whatever comes into his mind, in other words, to "brainstorm."

In most creative-thinking methods, from the most varied to the most sophisticated, we use the brainstorming as language. When we search out analogies, for example, we are brainstorming. When we use projective pictures, we are brainstorming; likewise when we make forced connections. When we let ideas emerge using the emergence technique, we are brainstorming. There is nothing special about the language of brainstorming: it is an application of the general principal of free association delineated by Jung and applied by Freud.

Brainstorming as Technique

Brainstorming is not only a language; it is also a technique for generating ideas, a technique whose formula is quite simple. In order to keep a group from evaluating, judging, weighing the pros and cons of, or repeatedly turning over in their heads an "original" idea before expressing it, brainstorming incites them to rapidly say whatever comes into their minds, "without thinking." **Rapidity** is the key to brainstorming.

The main characteristic of brainstorming is a "badam badam" rhythm akin to that of a boogie-woogie blues.

The mechanism of free association can also be performed at a slower pace, with each word, each image, each idea gradually appearing in fragments as out of a dense fog and which eventually coalesce, such as in wakeful dreaming or identification techniques. But in brainstorming, we play on rhythm, rapid association, perturbing the neural networks by thinking "faster than the music."

What makes brainstorming stand apart from other methods of creative thinking and detouring is not that of deferring judgment or free associating, which are common to all techniques; what makes it stand out is its use of rapidity to quantitatively generate ideas. This theory was first outlined by Guilford: *"the person who can produce the largest number of ideas in a given amount of time has a greater possibility, all other things being equal, of generating a larger number of possible solutions."*
There are three arguments that uphold this theory: the argument of the fundamental principle of statistics (creative accidents obey the law of probabilities); more technically, the argument that by generating a larger quantity of ideas we

facilitate the ability to make spontaneous connections between numerous stimuli; and the argument that a rapid, quantitative generation of ideas "stretches" the mind (as Stendhal wrote, "*I need three to four cubic feet of new ideas every day, as a steamboat requires coal*").

We could thus call brainstorming the "rapidity-quantity" technique, which is actually a more precise description since the word *brainstorming* used in a larger context can be applied to various other processes. We prefer to call it the "dynamic[12]" stance both to signify its rapidity and its energy.
Similarly, we could say that the dynamic stance correlates with the automatic writing of the Surrealist movement, or the brilliant, rapid, instantaneous improvisations of free jazz artists.

Brainstorming as language can be applied to other methods of idea generation as well. For example, you can break a problem down into its various components (a chair is composed of four legs, a seat, a back, etc.), its different functions (sit, rest, decorate, receive, etc.), and then deform all of these components in a "rapidity-quantity" manner to "fragment" the problem and generate solutions[13]. You could also make a forced connection between the problem and an exterior element or haphazard words, as recommended by De Bono, even an accident in a laboratory.

---

[12] See Guy Aznar and Stéphane Ely's book: *Ré-inventions, la démarche sensible de la créativité* (coming out in 2011).
[13] SCAMPER technique developed by Alex Osborn and Sid Parnes, who also developed Creative Problem Solving; the break down technique developed by the Synapse team and Guy Aznar in the 1970's.

Divergence and Convergence: the two creative Breaths of the Dynamic Stance

Stage 1: Divergence

In all creative problem-solving sessions, members of a group are asked to generate "ideas," whether realistic or unrealistic, reasonable or silly, adapted or crazy. This is the divergence phase, which in brainstorming and Creative Problem Solving, (developed by Osborn and Parnes) is described by the following rules: 1. *Look for novel, surprising ideas, 2. Defer judgment, 3. Generate quantity, 4. Connect the different ideas of the group.*

Its goal is to generate the greatest number of options[14].

In the divergence stage we allow ourselves to be carried along on a stream of free, rapid, multiform associations in order to break down automatic sequences and confuse the neural networks; neither the imagination nor deep thought is required. It is not truly projective and does not call on the unconscious except through rapid leaps or slips of the tongue.

Stage 2: Convergence

In this second stage we make a selection of ideas, fragments of ideas, suggestions. Several convergence methods are offered in the framework of Creative Problem Solving: evaluation, sorting, grouping (hits and highlights), and elaboration (PPCO

---

[14] As described by Olwen Wolfe in *J'innove comme on respire*, Editions du Palio, 2007.

technique, the target). Convergence, as described by Osborn and Parnes, is based on the following rules:

- Improve ideas: starting with a fragile idea, you can diverge again, enrich the idea, group several ideas into one.

- Judge affirmatively: search out what is compelling and positive about the idea, then—and only then—explore the criticisms and negative points with a desire to construct.

- Be deliberate: learn how to reject bad leads, be tenacious in your desire to transform each nascent idea into a potential solution and with the same level of energy for all ideas.

- Consider novelty (be daring!): explore the oddball ideas.

- Check with your objectives: reread the creative challenge frequently because all too often a problem-solving session leads to compelling ideas that do not necessarily respond to the initial objective.

"Dynamic" Stance

Rules of creative thinking during divergence and convergence

(CPS – Creative Problem Solving Osborn-Parnes)

Divergent thinking

Produce...

During the *divergence* phase, at the moment when ideas need to be produced and written down, it is essential to:

1. Defer judgment
2. Go for quantity
3. Let go ... seek original, surprising ideas
4. Combine, associate ideas
5. Write everything down

Convergent thinking

Be realistic, improve, strengthen....

During the *convergence* phase, it is essential to:

1. Improve ideas
2. Judge affirmatively
3. Be deliberate
4. Consider novelty
5. Check with your objectives

Dynamic Stance: Emblematic Techniques

The main emblematic tools used in the dynamic stance are:

Associative techniques: classic brainstorming, brain Post-its, brainwriting.

Deconstruction techniques: break down the problem, change functions, SCAMPER.

Confrontational techniques: collide, produce a shock, an encounter between two fields, establish a confrontational matrix, forced connections.

The Dynamic Stance: a Two-Stroke Engine

The concept of stages is key to the dynamic stance, a creative problem-solving method that unfolds in two **steps: 1) divergence 2) convergence (evaluate, sort, analyze)**. This two-step dynamic approach differs from the sensitive stance we will explore just below, which involves a third step: departure into an unfocused zone where creative emergence transpires.

The dynamic stance ("rapidity-quantity") is an approach to creative thinking that often produces brilliant results. It is practical and useful, demands little training, is well suited for certain problems, is adaptable to certain circumstances, and works well for certain people[15]. All creative-thinking coaches make use of it in their workshops.

But this dynamic stance is not the only creative-thinking strategy.

---
[15] There is ongoing research into these variables.

THE SENSITIVE STANCE IN THE PRODUCTION OF CREATIVE IDEAS

A Slow-Paced, Fuzzy, Intuitive Strategy

the "Sensitive" Stance

GUY AZNAR. STEPHANE ELY. JANUARY 2011

A Slow-Paced, Fuzzy, Intuitive Strategy: the "Sensitive" Stance, a Three-Stroke Engine

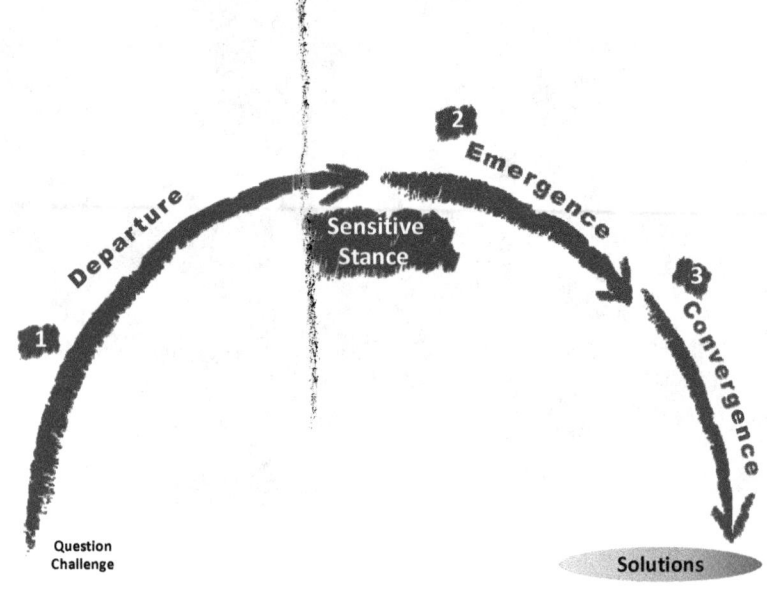

Here we have quite a different stance: one that is slow-paced, groping, and intuitive, and which we call the sensitive stance to highlight its emotional footing. This stance requires training, demands more time, is particularly suitable for certain problems and goals, and is complementary with the Dynamic Stance.

"Little Bicycle": the Language of the Sensitive Stance

If free association is the generic language of creative thinking, it is not always used identically. It depends on whether one is using a dynamic approach, associated with brainstorming, or a sensitive approach, with its process of immersion in images, which we call the "little bicycle[16]."

We have said that the dynamic stance is characterized by rapidity, energy, and generating quantity. Conversely, the sensitive stance is distinguished by its slow-paced rhythm. Here it is not a question of immediately producing new ideas, but that of sensations and images; an unhurried progression of images that slowly reveal themselves, much as a black and white image slowly appears on a piece of photo paper in a dark room. The rule of the game is to inhabit the imagination as a collective group experience, gradually allowing nascent ideas to take form that will then be translated into words. *"Imagine an object in front of you..."* and we wait for the object to appear. We don't try to come up with an imaginary story or simply express what the object brings to mind; we "watch" it reveal itself. Members of the group are urged to vocally express the fragments of images that come to them, which are then taken up by others who transform them, pass them on again, and so on, in a hovering, collective, imaginative atmosphere. The images should not be provoked, but allowed to slowly appear "out of the blue," then be translated into words.

This same exercise is performed following a projective activity, giving form to rough-hewn ideas through words with which the

---

[16] The expression "little bicycle" comes from an exercise we use at the beginning of our Sensitive Stance workshops, where we ask participants to "imagine a little bicycle." It has since become a part of our vocabulary.

group can then construct new, more developed ideas. This is the basic exercise we teach at the beginning of all our sensitive stance workshops, much as one would teach someone the basics of a new language before his visiting an unknown country..

We have come to call this exercise the "little bicycle" because,having frequently employed the phrase figuratively during our workshops, it has finally stuck. For example, we might begin a session with *"Imagine a child's bicycle... a little bicycle..."* ... *"Yeah, I see it. It's red..."* ... *"It's standing on the sidewalk..."* ... and the group takes off collectively on a quasi-hypnotic voyage. Later on, in the production stage, and depending on the situation, when we say, *"let's brainstorm"* or *"let's do the little bicycle exercise,"* everyone will understand what language rules apply. **Once the language has been absorbed, the sensitive path can be readily accessed.**

The sensitive path differs from the dynamic path in that it takes participants "further down the road," applying additional stages instead of instantly generating ideas. We are no longer following a two-step path (divergence - convergence) but a path that has three-steps:

1) Departure toward the imagination, allowing the unconscious free expression, entering a state between dream and wakefulness We shift the problem into the imagination.

2) We call the area of exploration where embryonic ideas emerge the **"emergence zone."** We steer the constraints of the problem toward the imagination, where we allow fuzzy, sketchy, fragmented ideas to emerge.

3) Transformation of unfocused ideas into solid, coherent ones during the **"convergence phase."** These ideas will later be passed through the filter of judgment, then evaluated in the process of their becoming operational solutions.

To explore this imaginative region we apply certain rules quite distinct from the "rapidity-quantity" approach and which we will touch on below. They include delayed writing, searching for hazy and imperfect ideas, and keeping a slow pace.

Example (*from Synectics: The Development of Creative Capacity*, W. J. J. Gordon (1961 - out of print)

The problem:
Subsequent to an airplane crash, you must solve a flight-instrument problem for the Aviation Ministry, which involves inventing an altimeter dial that eliminates mechanical and reading errors.

Imaginative thinking:
The engineer goes through a process of identification (excerpts from such a process): *"I am a coil in an altimeter... I expand... I contract... I'm stretched, then compressed... I feel squeezed... Someone's holding me by the feet, I'm being tortured... An altimeter dial without gears would be perfect... Stop looking for a solution, forget all that... Concentrate... I'm a coil in an altimeter, I expand then contract, how fatiguing..."*

Emergence
"I need an altimeter dial without gears, but how to move the needle on the dial without a coil... If it were to move linearly, along a tape... If I were a coil the size of a house... and I held on as it moved up and down ... what if I put a drop of ink on the coil... the ink would move inward when it contracted and outward when it expanded... if I put a drop of ink on the coil and then compress it, it draws an arc that is exactly the tape I need."

Elaborate
Following this stage, various diagrams are drawn up, followed by models that can then be tested by experts.

Departure, Emergence, Convergence: the Three Creative Breaths of the Sensitive Stance

Stage 1: Departure – Toward the Imagination

The word *departure* here signifies a "stepping back" from normal conscious thought and logical reasoning, much as a painter stands back from an easel. Departure evokes travel to a distance beyond: an unhurried journey to another country, planet, or the unknown. When the Imaginary is opposed to the Real, illogical to logical, folly to reason, the word *departure* suggests the idea of taking off, breaking the mooring lines, feeling queasy as you sail off to uncharted lands.

We could speak of "depth," of plunging into the subterranean waters of the imagination, the abyss of the unconscious. But the word *departure* as we intend it calls more to mind the virtue of taking flight toward the imagination that Bachelard[17] spoke of.
We go beyond divergence. We go beyond suspending judgment. We go beyond short-circuiting the rational mechanism with rapid thought. Basically, we try to enter into a distinct psychological state. We let go, as when we close our eyes and daydream, allowing images to flow by unsolicited, letting words ricochet off each other, inviting thoughts to roam aimlessly, even rambling to ourselves. We let go of the cautious, wise, conscious control of our words, our drawings, allowing the unconscious to take over.

---

[17] Gaston Bachelard, *Water and Dreams, Air and Dreams, The Psychoanalysis of Fire, Earth and Reveries of Will.*

This does not mean that we are required to make public what is private, or unveil our well-hidden inner secrets. We are talking here about a creative-thinking workshop, not a session with a psychoanalyst. Just as an artist translates his secret imaginative world into a piece of art, which will then be put on display, so the creative thinker translates his private imaginative world into nascent ideas. It is these unformed ideas, not the route taken to generate them nor the twists and turns along the way, that concern us.

Departure

Departure
Sliding into imagination, using the unconscious

During the departure phase, you must:

1. Look to go slowly

2. Let go, associate freely and visually

3. Share vague intuitions and new sensations

4. Immerse yourself in mental imagery

5. Be inspired without searching purposely

Why probe the unconscious?

Well certainly not at the behest of some foolhardy desire. We delve into the unconscious because it contains a considerable amount of valuable information, images, and sensations that have been buried in its depths since birth and perhaps even before. The unconscious is a veritable treasure trove!

As the word *unconscious* signifies, the information contained within it is not readily available to consciousness, both because we do avail ourselves of that information on a daily basis (and why burden ourselves…) and because all those bits of information are, much like the old things in Grandma's trunk up in the attic, faded, dusty, and forgotten — not to mention that we voluntarily suppress or discard some of them, or associate them with bad memories.

But the large quantity of information stored in the depths of the unconscious constitutes the raw material of future creations. Our job is to allow that information to "emerge," to bring that living matter into the primal light of creation.

To say that we make a departure from conscious thought signifies that we move toward a state of reverie in which the ideas generated are governed by uncontrollable, subconscious rules.

We say we enter into a dream, we don't flee it, because what we are striving to attain is not an absence but a presence-absence: an intermediary state between reality and dream. We want to leave behind constraints yet not forget them, ignore reality yet constantly feel its presence, be at once here and elsewhere — that is the creative challenge.

This altered state most closely resembles that moment when, waking up in the morning, we try to recall the dream we just had even as the tasks of the day ahead demand our attention. We lie there, our eyes closed, trying to hold on to the dream for as long as possible for fear that it will disappear the moment we open our eyes — which is often the case. In this altered state we try to locate and hold on to the emerging unconscious material even as it slowly vanishes; we try to float in that imaginative space at length. It is sometimes said that our best ideas come to us at night; nothing could be less true. They come to us when we are in that altered state, in the dusk between sleep and wakefulness, where the fragments of dreams swirl in our heads while the problems that preoccupy us tug on our sleeves.

Graham Wallas[18] describes this in-between state, this fuzzy, marginal zone with its vague contours in which we feel somewhat lost, as the *"fringe consciousness."*

In our dreams, in our fantasies, we can reshape reality; with a little reverie we can transform a car, a chair, a table. We can melt it, stretch it, change its form and color, have it enter then escape from a vase or Aladdin's lamp in a cloud of smoke, just as we can digitally alter an image on a screen in unending ways. It is this same faculty we use to solve problems.

"In the moment of inspiration," Ehrenzweig[19] writes, *"reality will appear to him super-real and intensely plastic. (...) It is the privilege of the artist to combine the ambiguity of dreaming with the tensions of being fully awake."*

---

[18] Graham Wallas, *The Art of Thought (out of print)*.
[19] Anton Ehrenzweig, *The Hidden Order of Art*.

The secret weapon of creation is flexibility (that's the key word), and with it comes the ability to reshape reality in that "fantasy" state. To skillfully navigate that shifting space "between two hydrous bodies" where the mind, in a semi-conscious state, freely roams, seeking to connect two distant matrixes ("*bisociation*" as Koestler[20] termed it), drawing them toward each other in an attempt to create points of encounter that we call the "gestation idea," or "nascent idea." We must learn to move fluidly between these two strata, to travel gracefully between the indistinct and the distinct.

If we steer too abruptly toward the imagination without setting any boundaries, simply playing a game of associations, we are only amusing ourselves imaginatively and not creating. If, in our impatience to hold out before us the coherent, finalized idea, we return too rapidly from that state, we run the risk of coming up empty-handed, paralyzed by other boundaries.

New ideas are not imaginary things, dispersing themselves in a play of associations, like a plume of smoke. Nor do they aspire to rapidly become a splendid object. They exist somewhere in an "in between." This "in between" is exactly the space of the symbolic, which by definition is the connecting point between the Imaginary and the Real. We refer to this space where ideas begin to surface as the territory of **"emerging ideas[21]"** — a space not unlike that held by the leading note, or "blue note," in a piece of music. *"The moment between order and disorder is the reign of delight,"* wrote Paul Valéry[22]. Let us describe this space for a moment.

---

[20] Arthur Koestler, *The Cry of Archimedes*.
[21] *L'émergence des idées*, paper written by the authors in the framework of the Training Certificate in Creativity, at Université Paris Descartes (France), 2009.
[22] Paul Valéry, *Préface aux Lettres Persane* in *Variété II*, Gallimard, 1930.

Stage 2: Emergence of Ideas

During the emergence stage, the creative thinker finds himself facing the complex task of superimposing his imaginative state on the limiting reality of the problem before him, two very differing forms. An obstinate opposition rages between these two forms or visions, much as the piece of a puzzle we try to place in the empty space before us refuses to yield -- perhaps the piece even belongs to another puzzle.

It is precisely in this conflictual space, which we call "crossing-over[23]," that the quality of a piece of art, the originality of an idea finds its voice.

Crossing-over involves conflict, which justifies the use of the expression (in the sense of crossing swords at the beginning of a duel) to illustrate this dialectic encounter[24] between the Imaginary and the Real, a forced encounter that must be established between the stimuli produced in the imagination and the obstacles encountered (nascent ideas and harsh reality) between disorder and order.

This conflict is also the expression of the subjective tendency to reorganize information following an **internal** psychological order (that of the unconscious) and the need to resolve an **external** problem, one posed by the client.

---

[23] The notion of "crossing-over" was presented by Guy Aznar in his book *La créativité dans l'entreprise*, Editions d'Organisation, 1971.
[24] Instead of dialectic, we could use the word "dialogic," coined by Edgar Morin. He describes dialogic as *"the complex unity between two complementary, rival, antagonistic logics, which nourish each other, complete each other and oppose each other."* According to him, in dialogic logic *"the antagonisms remain the driving force behind the complex phenomena, while the Hegelian dialectic transcends the contradictions in reference to a superior unity."* Edgar Morin, *Le complexus*, in *Complexité, vertiges et promesses*, Édition Le Pommier, 2006.

"The growth of new images in art and new concepts in science is nourished by the conflict between two opposing structural principles," wrote Ehrenzweig[25].

In our case, in order to seal a connection between the vague form sketching itself in his mind and the limitations of the problem before him, the creative thinker must proceed slowly and with caution. To produce a creative idea, he must allow its nascent form to flow from the imagination into the mold of the set problem. He must accept to let the constraints of the problem rise to the surface — caress his imagination — because any violent encounter would turn into an abrupt judgment: *"that's impossible, it won't work."*

"Positive transformation" is the golden rule of crossing-over. Criticism is not concealed; it is transformed into a pressure point that can be applied to finding the solution. In practice, the crossing-over trajectory can be compared to walking down a flight of stairs: it is done step by step, with each step constituting a new foraging for ideas.

The creator of "sensitive" ideas must visualize his "storehouse" of conscious and unconscious information globally in order to glimpse the various choices it has to offer. We are talking about a considerable quantity, an actual ocean of information in which one might easily drown.

As he flies over the vast territory, the creative thinker must be able to detect any telltale traces or forms, much as certain archeological signs can only be seen from an aerial view. Much like an image that breaks up into pixels as it is enlarged, the

---

[25] Anton Ehrenzweig, *op. cit.*

mechanisms that are put into practice as we depart toward the imagination work to break down the structure of the problem into millions of bits of information.

Now how do we create a new image, a new shape — in other words, a new idea — with all of these bits of information?

The creative thinker must consider a multitude of choices, flying over and detectng new forms in this chaotic universe. As Henri Laborit[26] wrote, "... *what characterizes the human race is the tools it possesses in the neocortex, which is responsible for higher-order cognitive functions. These tools allow us to construct new forms from the memory stored in the paleoencephalon.*"

The same imaginary stimulation, the same design, the same dream can generate a great number of ideas. Thus the importance during the emergence stage of foraging at length for the "outlines of fuzzy ideas," fragments of ideas, leads we can then explore. Thus the interest in keeping the emergence engine active as long as possible, tirelessly scanning the area in search of one form — or an idea — then another, without lingering on the first or the second, without lingering on the most attractive, determinedly pursuing the gathering of ideas, which later will be placed on a workbench to be sorted.

---

[26] Henri Laborit, *L'éloge de la fuite*, Poche, 1985.

The best creative thinker is the one who can let his gathering instinct scan the field at length, the one who can postpone ideas longer than others.

For an idea to emerge we must use our unconscious vision, take a step back, look for signs, uncover leads. There are no maps, no roads; the only solution is to navigate sensitively with our intuition: "*I feel...*" "*I feel*"...

This is the situation we must accept to enter into the emergence stage: we move forward like an alert hunter advancing through the forest, blindly following vague tracks, on the lookout for clues and signs in order to flush out a rare bird.

This technique of being "on the lookout" for ideas is one that we use in our creative-group workshops during the emergence stage.

It is important, in this stage, to consider the ideas generated during the departure stage (wakeful dreaming, identification, etc.) with the gaze of a hunter following the "leads" of ideas. We listen to a recording of the content that was generated bit by bit during the departure phase, ready to stop each time a member of the group intuitively feels a lead (an idea, a word, a phrase). Group members lie down on the floor with their eyes closed and listen, exploring a multitude of "crossings-over." When someone says, "Stop, I have a lead," the others turn their attention on him, like rugby players in a scrum, to urge him forward and help him follow his intuition. The fragmented idea is written down, to be referred to later on, and the group again begins its search for another imaginary stimulus.

To help the exploration of the emergence zone, we have put in place a set of rules, different from those used in the dynamic stance.

Defer ideas

Experience shows that this intermediate zone between the Imaginary and the Real that we have just described is a region where anxiety reins, where participants feel off balance and are often provoked to rapidly seize on an "idea." When we generate an idea we produce a solid object, like a life buoy, so as not to drown in the uncertainty felt as the unconscious pulls us under and as "solid ground" voices its judgment.

But when we rush to define an idea, we restrict those evanescent, vague, moving forms, interrupting their fluidity, "cutting them off," and surely killing any emerging idea. We have barely glimpsed the idea struggling to emerge and are still partially held in the short-circuiting attitude of the divergence stage, the process of crossing-over with its various constraints having only been initiated and reality having scarcely been grazed.

Similarly, when we awake from a dream and hurriedly try to write it down, we stop its evolution. The incentive to rush to record a nascent idea lessens its wealth just when it should be given time to evolve by simply "staying with it." Expressions such as "I feel something," "I have an intuition," "I have a vague feeling," "I feel... I feel..." can aid this process.

Furthermore, if we try to convert imaginative material too rapidly, we congeal it and decrease the number of possibilities. The imaginative visual form, the drawing, the fragment of dream that has caught our attention and that we see before us could potentially contain numerous ideas and not just one. There is often a mine of ideas in one single imaginary stimulus. The act of announcing the result too rapidly, of holding the winning idea up to the light, pushes others ideas off to the side.

Thus it is important to slow down the process, proceeding almost in slow motion. This is the essential point, the number one rule of the emergence stage.

If the dynamic strategy is based on the principle of "**deferring judgment**" (and quite rightly so since it is the absence of judgment that allows for the burst of divergence), the emergence stage is based on the principle of "**deferring ideas**."

Speak with metaphors and poetry

It is not as easy as it might seem to become skillful at "deferring ideas." We are used to the "rules" of brainstorming: generate ideas, rapidly, without thinking, quality is found in quantity,… etc. For it to be mastered, "postponing ideas" requires training, a motive, an argument.

One of the keys is to have the group talk in metaphors. We make use of metaphor, in this case, not to diverge from an idea so vague that we have difficulty clearly formulating it, but to decipher it. James Clerk Maxwell wrote that the electromagnetic field acted like a *"collection of wheels, pulleys and fluids"*; Planck spoke of N particles that behaved like oscillators, as if they were *"connected by springs"* ; Kekulé discovered the ring shape of the benzene molecule after day-dreaming of a serpent eating its own tail ; Einstein imagined sitting astride a ray of light in order to explain what takes place when traveling at the speed of light.

Metaphor, or poetic description, aids us in deciphering new ideas without restricting them by hasty, formal commentary. It also allows others to "enter into the idea" as it presents itself, and to understand it intuitively.

Search for hazy and imperfect Ideas[27]

During the emergence stage, a creative-thinking group should never be asked to express clear, precise, fixed ideas. They should be invited instead to produce shards, fragments, specters, rough-hewn ideas, sketches of ideas. They should be asked to offer ideas as yet barely distinguishable because, to begin with, no one ever comes up with a completely ready-made idea, and, more importantly, when we expect someone to offer a polished idea, a clear concept, we oblige them to turn their attention to the act of judging, evaluating, finalizing.
In contrast, we are interested here in exploring an intermediate zone, a space between shadow and light.

"The flawless curve of a 'finished' idea evokes a polished, impenetrable surface... It can be either true or false... It no longer offers itself to improvement... On the contrary, rough-hewn ideas, with their cracks and crevices, are open to creative intervention..." wrote Didier Anzieu[28].

---

[27] Two creative workshop trainers (Guillemette Goglio and Mathilde Sarré Charrier) researched the notion of the "fuzzy" and the "slow-pace" of the emergence stage for a assignment in one of the theoretical classes of the Training Certificate in Creativity in 2009. Following their research they wrote a paper whose summary can be found on the Créa-Université website (www.crea-univ.fr).

[28] Didier Anzieu, *Le corps de l'œuvre*, Gallimard, 1981.

Keep going Slowly

In his book *Hare Brain, Tortoise Mind, Why Intelligence Increases When You Think Less*[29], Guy Claxton identifies two modes of thought, which he calls *fast thinking* and *slow thinking*:

"The first is rational, analytic, linear, logical," he writes. *"It operates when we react under pressure, when we are pressed for time. (...) Slow thinking is intuitive, primitive, creative. It comes into play when we are no longer under pressure and have the time to let ideas come to light at their own rhythm. Scanners show that these two modes of thought produce different brain waves (the slower alpha and theta waves during slow thinking, and the more rapid beta waves during fast thinking)..."*

The dynamic stance promotes a rapid, quantitative generation of ideas, which is a totally legitimate approach. Rapid generation breaks down the vague desire to make judgment, leaves no time for evaluation, and favors a continuous fountain of association. It is indispensable in divergence.

Conversely, in the departure and emergence stages, a slower-paced rhythm is called for. When we are unhurried we can take the time to wander through the twists and turns of our imagination, to daydream, searching a form perhaps glimpsed yet not absorbed. This state could be considered close to that of meditation. Anzieu[30] calls it *"the creative shock"*:
"The characteristic feature of the creative shock is the sense of a floating of the limits that separate the different levels..."

---

[29] Guy Claxton, *Hare Brain, Tortoise Mind, Why Intelligence Increases When You Think Less*, Fourth Estate, London, 1997.
[30] Didier Anzieu, *op. cit.*

When we are calm we can enter into a state of diffuse attention with less effort, a state "where all of our senses are awakened." In this intermediate stage we virtually spin the configurations of information, images, the fragile, fuzzy, ephemeral ideas that we almost dare not name. Think of the kaleidoscopes of childhood into which we peered to discover a multi-colored flower that, as we slightly turned the cardboard cylinder, changed into another flower, then another, at once the same and yet of a different color, another style. That is how the configurations of nascent ideas compose and recompose themselves.

Searching for an idea is not that different from detective work. We sniff around, uncover clues, track down leads, construct theories... Then suddenly all the elements of the perceptive field coalesce, and an idea begins to profile itself before our eyes. We are profilers of ideas.

THE SENSITIVE STANCE IN THE PRODUCTION OF CREATIVE IDEAS

Emergence

Emergence

Let the idea appear, let it surface...

During the emergence phase, you must:

1. Defer ideas and delay writing
2. Speak with metaphors and poetry
3. Search for hazy and imperfect ideas
4. Keep going slowly

... followed by the « sensitive » convergence phase

Stage 3: "Sensitive" Convergence

Once the ideas have emerged, it is time to embark on the path of convergence.

The "sensitive" convergence stage is quite similar to the "dynamic" convergence stage. However, the nature of ideas that emerge in the sensitive stance often require a more meticulous and unhurried approach so as not to perturb the subtleties, imaginative charge, and implicit originality of the nebulous idea that has just emerged[31].

Instead of grouping ideas into clusters, following a coherent logic, as is done is the dynamic process, we proceed differently:
- We create clusters following subjective, intuitive criteria[32] (see intuitive cluster guidelines)
- We seize on an idea without trying to class it in a cluster (see hits and highlights called "on the fly" guidelines)
- We enrich the vein of ideas by exploring it imaginatively, using the "little bicycle" language (see sensitive development of clusters guidelines).

---

[31] For her dissertation at Créa-Université, Nathalie Portolan worked on an analysis of different groupings and *clusterings* related to specific techniques. She suggested that, in order to preserve the potential richness of an emerging idea, the "sensitive" *clustering* phase should be particularly slow-paced.
[32] Isabelle Jacob describes, for example, the "favorite selection" technique in an article published in the Créa-France newsletter, November 2009.

Sensitive Stance: Emblematic Techniques

Projective techniques: projective identification using a collection of abstract images, figurative and symbolic props, spontaneous drawings, personal items and collages not necessarily related to the subject, point-and-shoot photos, natural and urban environments, etc.

Graphic techniques: illustrations, individual drawings, collective drawings, frescos, clay modeling, constructed objects (models, sculptures), photos, collages, etc.

Dream-related techniques: dreaming of an ideal solution; emptying the mind; meditation, imaginary stories, wakeful dreaming (individually and collectively); plots; symbolism in fairytales; dreaming of sensations, perfumes, music, touch; imaginary trips; magician's box[33]...

The Sensitive Stance, a Three-Stroke Engine

The Sensitive Stance calls voluntarily on the imagination in a three-stage approach.

1) In the first stage, we let go and **depart toward the imagination**, generating stimulating imaginative thoughts or clues.

---

[33] A technique of saturation and formulation of dreams and desires inspired by psychodrama. Developed by René Bernèche (Professor of Psychology of Creative Behavior, Montreal, Quebec).

2) In the second stage, after "crossing-over" the generated material with the components of the problem, **we allow nascent ideas to emerge.**

3) In the third stage, during **a sensitive convergence stage**, we begin to transform the emerging ideas into solutions.

The three stages of this stance create one of the major differences with the dynamic stance, which, as we have seen, generates ideas in two stages (divergence, convergence).

THE SENSITIVE STANCE IN THE PRODUCTION OF CREATIVE IDEAS

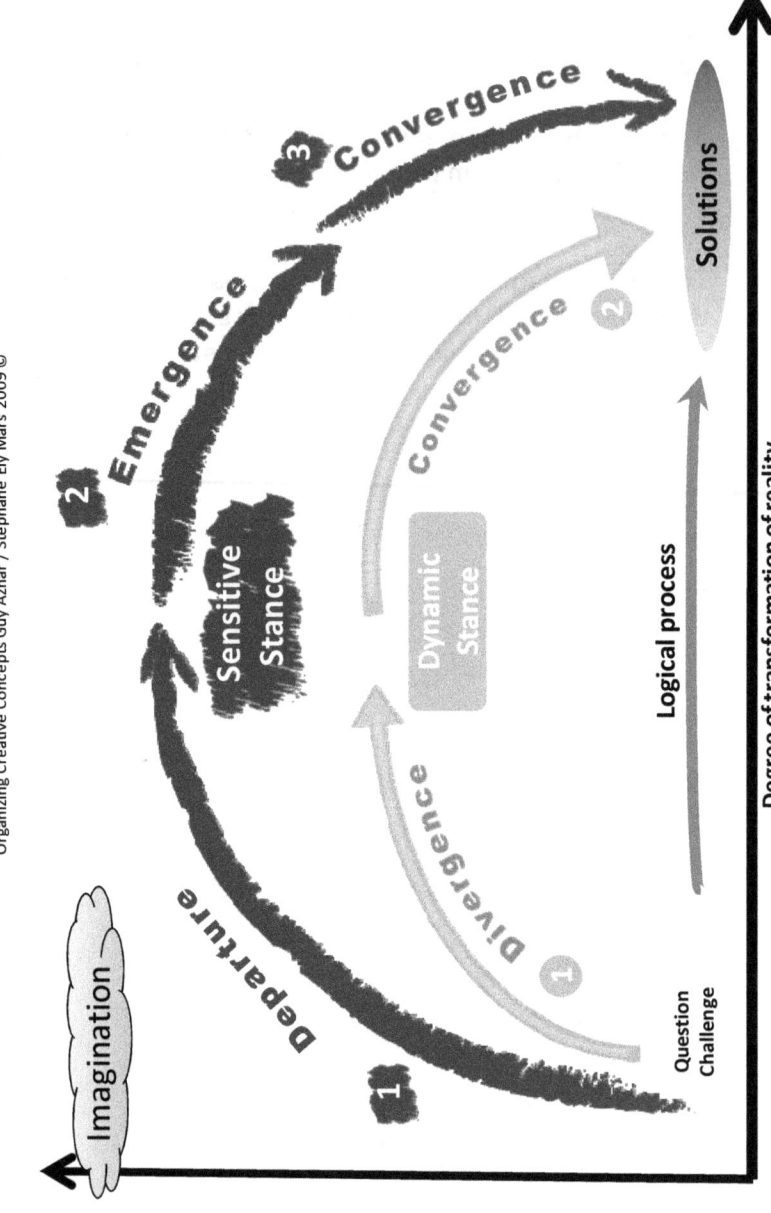

III. Links between Creativity, Energy, and Emotion

The Role of Energy in the Creative Process

Why does creative thinking expend such energy?

First, because creative, unfamiliar actions consume more energy, while uncreative, repetitive actions economize energy. The greater the innovation, the greater the expenditure of energy, particularly if it goes against our customs, principles, usages, traditions, and the advantages gained through inertia.

Second, because a greater quantity of energy is expended when we delve into the "irrational" unconscious than when we stand on firm, familiar ground. Even if this step is temporary and accomplished in a secure, supervised setting, moving toward the unconscious is risky business. Logical reasoning was invented to give reassurance, to organize disorder, to devise paths through the jungle. Here we are being asked to return to the unfocused, disorganized thought of the primitive, of the child. When we express irrational ideas in front of a group, we are taking a risk that goes beyond the possibility of being judged by one's social group, which explains why we spend so much time developing confidence in our groups.

Third, and on a deeper level, we reveal more about ourselves during the creative process. To throw out ideas without holding back or limiting our words to what is considered socially acceptable is certainly risk-taking; it demands a certain energetic output and assumes a certain confidence in the group.

Origin of the Energy in the Creative Process

Human energy is by nature emotional. *"No emotion, no life,"* as David Servan Schreiber[34] wrote. The word *emotion* comes from the Latin verb *motere*, which means to stir, and the prefix *e*, which designates a movement toward the exterior. Emotion and motivation come from the same linguistic root. And to take that first step down any path, we must be motivated, filled with desire or animosity, passion or anxiety — in short, filled with emotion. To move, we must be moved!

It was Piaget who emphasized the two aspects of human behavior, feelings and intelligence: *"...'feelings' and 'intelligence' are simply behavior relating to persons and behavior affecting ideas or things (...) each behavioral transformation is both affective and cognitive."*[35]

The involvement of the emotions in the creative process is essential for several reasons.

Firstly, our emotions are a storehouse of a different kind of memory. When recalling a dream from the night before or suddenly having an unexpected idea, we often ask ourselves, *Where did that come from?* It would be like a computer having two memories: the regular memory used for sending emails and a mysterious memory that at times must be tracked down. Secondly, our emotional memories tend to flock together in a more nimble, haphazard manner, enhancing our chances of generating novel ideas.

---

[34] David Servan Schreiber, *The Instinct to Heal*.
[35] Jean Piaget, *The Psychology of the Child*, *The Psychology of Intelligence*, *The Representation of the World in the Child*.

Todd Lubart[36], who has conducted several research projects on the link between emotion and creativity, has shown that when we access our emotions we increase our innovative ability to interpret stimuli, and that emotional experiences collaborate in our establishing links between two concepts theoretically opposed yet emotionally supportive.

Franck Zenasni has researched how our emotions stimulate creativity depending on whether they are negative, as in seeking an idea to resolve a worrisome situation, or positive, as in improving our well-being[37].

But it must be acknowledged that emotional excess of any kind thoroughly unsettles the mind; thus our emotions must be regulated through rational analysis, which is the realm of the cognitive mind. Our mental life, as noted by Professor Damasio[38], is the result of a constant interaction between our affective and cognitive processes. This interaction is precisely what we try to promote by alternating the divergence-departure-emergence stages with those of convergence.

---

[36] Todd Lubart, Research Professor at Université René Descartes (France) and author of *Psychologie de la créativité* (*op. cit.*).
[37] Journal of Individual Differences, 2008, Vol 29, page 157.
[38] Antonio Damasio, American researcher, cited by David Servan Schreiber (*op. cit.*).

Emotional Involvement in the Creative Process

How to Mobilize Emotion: the Group as Vehicle of Emotion

To mobilize his emotions when called upon to create, the inventor uses various "techniques": rituals and recipes, multiple and varied habits, silence or noise, chosen times, favorite stimulations (even artificial ones).

In the context of this book, we would like to generate ideas in a less complex manner (creativity is not the stuff of magic), a more democratic manner (we are all creative thinkers), as well as a more practical manner (the context being that of companies and institutions).

In order to accomplish this, we turn to the creative-thinking group: a working unit that, instead of consuming energy, produces it — while providing a safe, secure setting that allows participants to involve their emotions (on the condition of having previously attended a group workshop and learned the appropriate stimulation techniques). The members of a creative-thinking group must be able to communicate flawlessly with each other, as if they were one person with ten heads all soliloquizing, or a single person with ten different memory storehouses offering the prospect of ten associative-thought processes, each able to move fluidly from one to the other, able to perceive what the other is about to say, much as we sense the tip of an idea appearing in our own minds. Though this is the stuff of myths, we must urge ourselves to draw as near as possible to this environment.

The stimulation process used to get the emotional engine going will vary depending on whether we are in a dynamic or sensitive stance.

The Playful Emotional Engine of the Dynamic Stance

In the dynamic stance, the emotional engine is of a playful nature. To create a relaxed atmosphere, the coach will ask a group to do a few fun stretching exercises, called *"icebreakers."* Osborn spoke of *"creating the atmosphere of a picnic":* a stimulating, often joyful ambiance in which the codes of politeness are broken down, the rules of logic set aside, and judgment temporarily suspended.

The More Intense, Authentic Emotional involvement of the Sensitive Stance

Here the group has presumably attended in-depth creative-group workshops. We use *"icebreakers"* as well as other exercises that we call "involvers," which bring the emotions more deeply into play.

It is useful if the group has also attended a non-verbal communication workshop involving body movement, gesture, graphic, and sound exercises. Paradoxically, it is when we encourage silence within the group that communication among the members improves. We accomplish this by having them do a series of exercises that we call "non- verbal exercises." These are essentially physical exercises, expressive performances that go from everyday gestures to rhythmic movements, even dance, and that bring into play a whole series of corporeal expressions.

Earlier in the workshop we might have done several psychological "regulations," where we ask the different participants to express how they feel within the group and with each other, drawing up a sort of emotional sociogram, the object being to transform the group into what Kurt Lewin[39] calls *"a dynamic system, a state of balanced forces."*

---

[39] Kurt Lewin, *Principles of Topological Psychology*, MacGraw Hill, 1936.

IV. The Solution Finding Process

Creativity can spread over all the stages of the process

The dynamic and sensitive stances can spread over all the stages of the solution finding process.

The process of creative thinking that we described above should not be confused with the complex mechanism used in resolving problems, which requires the production of projects ready to be implemented.

Whether we use a "two-stroke engine" or a "three-stroke engine," the process that we have just spelled out aims at **generating ideas** through a familiarization with the psychological mechanisms of creativity.

To **produce solutions** involves quite another strategy. In this instance we progress along a structured itinerary that must be methodically adhered to and that consists of three universally accepted conceptual stages, known since the time of Archimedes.

The Dynamic and Sensitive Stances can spread over all the stages of the Solution Finding Process

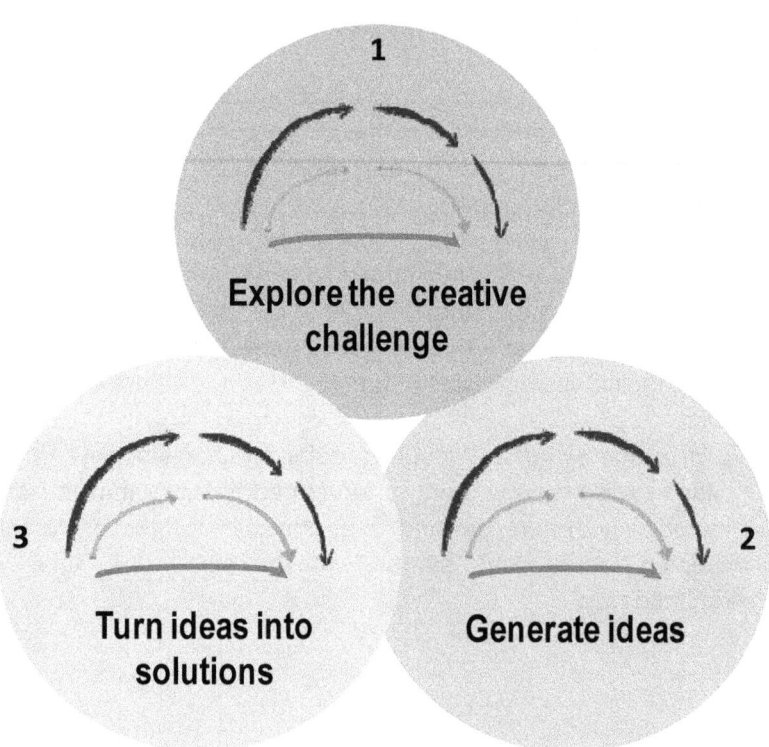

1. Explore the creative challenge
2. Generate ideas
3. Turn ideas into solutions

The 3 meta-stages of the Solution-Finding Process

A) **Explore the creative challenge**

B) **Propose possibilities or generate ideas by whatever means**

C) **Make a selection, develop, then implement the solutions**

What is so intelligent and original about the method explored by Sidney J. Parnes and Alex Osborn, and developed over the last fifty years by workshop coaches trained at the Creative Problem Solving Institute in Buffalo, NY, is the way the creative thought is inserted into each stage of the problem-solving process.

We would like to emphasize this essential fact: the act of creative thinking in the sensitive or dynamic detour is applied not only in the second, idea-generating stage. It spreads over all the stages of the process. The dynamic and sensitive stages, either alone or in combination depending on the coach's style, can be used to embark more creatively upon the path that leads to achievable solutions. Whether it is stage A (where we explore the challenge), stage B (where we generate a quantity of ideas), or stage C (where we turn ideas into solutions), we inject creative energy into each step.

Formulating the challenge is a creative task that can be interpreted as either dynamic or sensitive.

To transform emerging ideas into concrete solutions, to concentrate on those that seem workable, and to sidestep objections, require creativity and ideas.

Creative thinking is a skill that must be carried out in a repetitive fashion during each step of the problem-solving process, and it is an essential ingredient of that process. We could compare creating a solution to a problem to performing a complex piece of music in which several musicians play their parts throughout the various movements, from the andante to the final allegro; this would be one interpretation of the music in either a dynamic or sensitive style.

The creative problem-solving process has been described in various ways over the years, depending on the author and the period of time, and in some methods the three meta-stages have been divided into several sub-stages. Graham Wallas[40], for example, one of the pioneers in the field of the creative imagination and often cited as a reference, outlined four stages: preparation, incubation, illumination, and verification[41]. Let us point out that in stage 2 *"where there is no conscious thinking of the problem"* and in stage 3 *"where the creative idea bursts forth,"* Wallas comes close to our distinction between the imaginary departure and the emergence of the idea.

William J. J. Gordon[42], the author of *Synectics*, describes a nine-stage process.

---

[40] Graham Wallas, *op.cit.*
[41] Preparation *(where the problem is explored)* corresponds with stage 1; incubation *(where the problem is put aside)* and illumination *(where the new idea emerges)* can be considered as sub-phases of stage B; and verification *(the idea is tested and elaborated)* corresponds to stage C.

[42] William J. J. Gordon, *op. cit.*

The Standard Reference Process: Creative Problem Solving

The current standard reference to creatively solving problems, which has become as generic as brainstorming to generating ideas, is the Osborn-Parnes Creative Problem Solving model, which contains three mega-stages that can be subdivided into several steps.

In her wonderfully rigorous and pedagogic work, Olwen Wolfe[43] distinguishes eight phases within the three meta-stages of the CPS method.

**Sequences in Creative Problem Solving
Osborn-Parnes Method**

1. Explore the challenge	2. Generate ideas and solutions	3. Turn solutions into actions
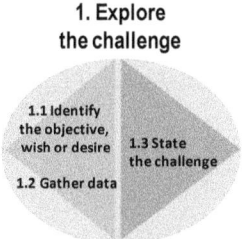	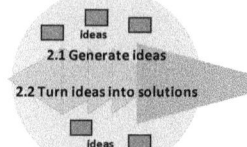	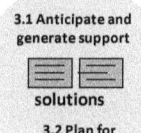
Discern "what is the challenge?"	**Produce** "materialise ideas and turn them into solutions"	**Make feasible** "turn a solution into actions"
Identify The basis, the subjective perception of the problem. **Collect** Compile and look at what exists. **Express** Voice what you want to change and what is problematic. State the creative challenge.	**Take some distance** Release your creativity, and draw up a list of ideas as long as possible. **Find solutions:** Observe, group, reinforce and select the main ideas and imagine how they could work and become solutions.	**Turn solutions into actions** **Plan the action:** Once a solution is chosen, draw up a roadmap. A solution is mainly a project with operational planning and the means to impose it.

---

[43] Olwen Wolfe, *J'innove comme on respire*, Editions du Palio, 2007.

Every year for the past fifty-five years, the CPSI has held a conference at which it presents its most recent theories on how best to implement the creative problem-solving process. We organize a similar event in the framework of the Créa-Université Association, in conjunction with our "sensitive" stance training programs.

The Three Meta-Steps of the Solution-Finding Process from the Perspective of the Sensitive Stance

A) Explore the Challenge
In this first stage, the original problem is formulated, its environment explored (ecosystem), the challenge absorbed, points of entry highlighted, the creative challenge articulated and then reformulated.

In addition to a mainly logical approach, we also use creative techniques, both dynamic and sensitive, to define and reformulate the challenge, assimilate it, take a step back from it and observe it from a different angle. In addition to a dynamic approach, we can also use a sensitive approach to lead several paths in this stage. We are not so much trying to formulate the problem as trying to observe it imaginatively and sensitively, opening it up, shining a different light on it in order to better capture its essence and sense.

B) Generate Ideas responding to the creative challenge
It is during this stage that the creative process truly comes into play with the generation of creative ideas. This phase draws on the many solid techniques, from the most dynamic to the most sensitive, in order to awaken the imagination.

C) Turn Ideas into Concrete Solutions
In this stage, alongside a logical approach, we use creative techniques to transform ideas into solutions, prepare the field

for their acceptance, multiply their chances for a successful application, and optimize the course of action.

Several dynamic techniques can be used here; for example, sorting the ideas by color[44], or grouping them ("hits and highlights" technique). These groupings, called "clusters," can then be amplified in different ways: either with elaboration and optimization techniques, such as PPCO (develop and refine the idea by pointing out its Plusses, Potentials, Concerns, and Options); or by writing concept boards; or by having the client choose one idea from among those offered and thus determine the desired direction to take; or by a combination of these different ways.

This dynamic approach can be completed with or replaced by a sensitive approach, such as with the "little bicycle" exercise, providing more latitude to the imagination in the choice and elaboration of the ideas that will become solutions.

The emblematic techniques of the sensitive stance are presented in the appendix.

---

[44] Mark Raison distinguishes four families of color: blue ideas (simple ideas easy to put into practice, easily accepted); green ideas (those that improve a current situation and develop it); red ideas (those that create a rupture, a radical change, while still seeming feasible); and yellow ideas (surprising, improbable ideas that introduce a radical rupture; these are visionary, dream-like, and fascinating, which might move us to say: *It seems impossible, but let's try it!*)

Sensitive Stance

a. Slowness
b. Melody
c. Smoldering fire, bubbling lava
d. Letting go
e. Receptivity
f. Fuzzy, fragmented ideas
g. Hesitate, slow pace, sensitive
h. Exploration, discovery, navigation
i. Plumb the unconscious
j. Roam, tinker, loose yourself
k. Symbolic references: preferably Yin, Dionysian, water, air

Strong emotional implication

- Methodic emotional reinforcement, mobilization of group dynamic
  ✓ Register of exercises implicating emotion
  ✓ Corporeal implication
  ✓ Emotional "regulations" (how do I feel in the group)

Dynamic Stance

a. Rapidity
b. Rhythm
c. Explosion
d. Tension
e. Attention
f. Clear ideas, complete ideas
g. Determination
h. Quantity
i. Consciousness (or unconsciousness produced by accident, an intentional or unintentional "slip")
j. Follow a plan
k. Symbolic references: preferably Yang, Apollonian, earth, fire

Low emotional involvement

✓ Turning emotion into playful, festive involvement; emotion under control
✓ Register of ice breakers
✓ No physical touch
✓ Debriefing as opposed to emotional regulation

Creative breath

Sensitive Three-Stroke Engine
Departure / Emergence / Sensitive Convergence (Aznar/Ely)

- **Departure**
  - Look to go slowly
  - Let go, associate freely and visually
  - Share vague intuitions and new sensations
  - Immerse yourself in mental imagery
  - Be inspired without searching purposely

- **Emergence**
  - Defer ideas and delay writing
  - Speak with metaphors and poetry
  - Search for hazy and imperfect ideas
  - Keep going slowly

- **Sensitive Convergence**
  - Trust your intuition
  - Elaborate with "little bicycle" language
  - Dynamic convergence

Dynamic two-stroke engine
Divergence / Convergence (Osborn Parnes)

- **Divergence**
  - Defer judgment
  - Go for quantity
  - Let go ... seek original, surprising ideas
  - Combine, associate ideas
  - Write everything down

- **Convergence**
  - Improve ideas
  - Judge affirmatively
  - Be deliberate
  - Consider novelty
  - Check with your objectives

Related techniques and tools

Techniques specific to the sensitive stance

- **Projective Techniques:** identification, use of projective props.
- **Dream-related Techniques:** dream the ideal solution; empty your head; storytelling (individual or collective); plots; fairytale symbolism, imaginary travels, awake dreaming

Techniques that can be used in both dynamic and sensitive stances

- **Analogical techniques:** analytical, logical or intuitive, metaphors, parables, etc.
- **Outside-the-box techniques:** naïve gaze, childlike gaze, a different perspective.
- **Graphic techniques:** construction of objects (models, sculptures), photos, collages, etc.

Techniques specific to the dynamic stance

- **Associative techniques:** classic brainstorming, brain post-it, brain writing
- **Deconstructive techniques:** break up the problem, change functions... SCAMPER
- **Confrontational techniques:** clash, produce a shock, meet "in-between," establish confrontational guidelines... forced connections

In conclusion

A New Look at Emergence

The concept of the emergence of ideas is neither an arbitrary, artificial, novel, or supplemental concept suddenly pulled out of a hat: the emergence stage is one that all inventors and creators of ideas inevitably pass through regardless of the method employed, and generally without recognizing or clearly being aware of it. Like Monsieur Jourdain[45], each of us brings ideas to the surface without being conscious of the process; when we create, we all pass through the emergence stage.

If it has been our desire to highlight this concept of the emergence of ideas, it is precisely to call attention to this sensitive space, to zoom, as with a lens, into this territory we normally pass through at the speed of light, taking our time to savor the uncertainty, which leads us to suddenly uncover a clue, a path leading in semidarkness to discovery.

We have examined the sensitive stance here in the hopes of developing, teaching, and promoting this approach.

The emergence stage is precisely THE symbolic phase of creative thinking; the stages preceding it are preparatory, while those following it are used for giving a shape and refining.

---

[45] Monsieur Jourdain is a famous character created by Molière, notably in his play *The Bourgeois Gentleman*. Monsieur Jourdain wishes to acquire social skills, so he employs, among others, a Philosophy Master. During his lessons, the Philosophy Master trains him to speak in verses (versus prose). So Monsieur Jourdain suddenly discovers that he has been speaking prose all his life and didn't even know it!

Dynamic and Sensitive: Two Complementary Stances

It would not be difficult to pit the "American school of creative thinking" with its brainstorming against the "French school of creative thinking" with its projective detour, its slower-paced methods, and its emotional engagement. However, that is not what we wanted to develop here.

Osborn's brainstorming obviously corresponds with the pragmatic, simple, and direct operational aspects of American culture. Moreover, it was popularized more than fifty years ago in the Creative Problem Solving Process (CPS), developed in the framework of the Creative Education Foundation thanks to Sidney J. Parnes, and now taught by numerous talented American coaches.

The sensitive stance obviously corresponds to the European culture, and more particularly the French culture, developed by, among others, Anzieu and Rorschach in projective techniques, Carl Jung and Robert Desoille in the waking dream, by Gianni Rodari in his grammar of fantasy, and Bachelard in his symbolic meanings of the four elements. It was put into practice by Synapse[46] in 1966, giving rise to studies in qualitative projective techniques and spawning an ever-growing family of French creative-thinking coaches.

But the contrast between the two schools is not so clear.

---

[46] Synapse is the name of the first French creative-thinking institute, created by Guy Aznar, Christian Aznar and Pierre Bessis in 1966, spearheading studies in this field. Numerous creative-thinking coaches working today graduated from the "Synapse school." The Synapse method is explored in the book *La créativité dans l'entreprise* by Guy Aznar, Editions d'Organisation, 1971.

The sensitive stance was also initiated by the American William J.J. Gordon, who developed his slow-paced creative process Synectics[47] by asking a patient during his psychoanalysis to verbalize his imaginative thoughts and by outlining the identification technique, an important aspect of the emergence phase.

Back when the Creative Problem Solving Institute (CPSI) first came into being, Sid Parnes spent long hours studying projective techniques and the harnessing of the emotions[48].
Today, in the United States, numerous practitioners and researchers employ projective techniques to enhance their production, and recent university articles (notably Harvard publications) have cited the method. On the flip side, a growing number of researchers in France and Europe are using the rapid dynamic approach, at times ignoring all together the stages of the sensitive stance.

The truth of the matter is that, all cultural differences aside, the two stances are quite complementary. Ideally, both stances should be mastered, enabling one to turn to the dynamic stance for certain problems and to the sensitive stance when wanting to probe the imagination more deeply, or even using both of them at different stages in the search for a creative solution.

---

[47] An invented word that stands for a "combination of heterogeneous elements," a crossing-over or bisociation.
[48] Other researchers have expanded on his research, notably René Bernèche (Professor of Psychology of Creative Behavior, Montreal, Quebec), who outlined a model stressing the links between concepts, mental imagery, perceptions, and sensations. This passionate work highlights the links between emotions, ideas, and concepts in the creative-thinking process.

The Sensitive Stance is a creative engine that can be integrated into the CPS process, incorporating new approaches and adding to its enrichment.

A University Training Certificate in Creativity to Deepen Understanding of the Creative Process

The University Training Certificate in Creativity, introduced by Todd Lubart and Guy Aznar at Université Paris Descartes in France[49], aims to offer an impartial synthesis of the various methods of creative expression, open to all schools of thought, and to encourage on-going research in the field so as to deepen our knowledge of the creative mechanisms.

Paris, January 2010.
© Guy Aznar and Stéphane Ely

---

[49] Visit our website: www.crea-univ.com

V. Annexes

A Few Sensitive Techniques

In order to illustrate our topic, we have compiled a few emblematic techniques that are used in the different stages of the sensitive "three-stroke engine" approach. They have been specifically adapted to its creative steps.

Family 1: Departure Techniques for Imaginative Thinking

Family 2: Crossing-over Techniques for the Emergence of Ideas

Family 3: Sensitive Convergence Techniques for the Elaboration of ideas

All of these techniques can be used in the three meta-step framework of the creative problem-solving process. To help in understanding these techniques, keep in mind that in each of these meta-steps we search for:

- Ideas that express the creative challenge
- New ideas generated in the step "generate ideas" (!)
- Ideas that turn those previously generated into solutions and reinforce acceptance and application.

Family 1: Departure Techniques for Imaginative Thinking

Departure is associated with "standing back," much as a painter does when standing in front of his ease. Departure is associated with voyaging to far-off lands. The word *departure* suggests going a step farther, breaking anchor, going out of one's depth, traveling to unfamiliar places, letting go as in day-dreaming, where images flow by unhindered, words ricochet off one another, thoughts are fuzzy and indistinct.

"Little Bicycle"

Identification

Metaphors

Non-verbal techniques (drawings, corporeal movement)

Projective techniques

Practical Guide: "Little Bicycle"

The word *brainstorming* covers both language (a way of speaking) and technique (a manner of tackling problems). The sensitive stance differs from brainstorming in both language and approach.

Brainstorming is characterized by:
- Rapidity (which is not anecdotal, but strategic, in that it blurs analytical thinking)
- Deferred judgment
- Free-association
- Encouragement of the quantitative generation of ideas — any and every idea, even the most absurd
- A playful, dynamic group atmosphere

The language of the sensitive stance (which we call the language of the "little bicycle[50]") is often in conflict with that of brainstorming because:
- It promotes a slower pace.
- It is based on the association and combining of images, not words.
- It facilitates unconscious projections with the aid of projective techniques.
- It promotes the generation of imaginative material that will be transformed into ideas in a later stage, thus "deferring ideas."
- It encourages an involved emotional environment rather than a playful environment.

---

[50] The expression "little bicycle" comes from an exercise we use at the beginning of our Sensitive Stance workshops, where we ask participants to "imagine a little bicycle." It has since become a part of our vocabulary.

Objectives

"Thinking in images" is key to the departure toward the imagination. Whereas words are symbolic and correspond to a higher level of intelligence, images, like dreams, are a more archaic mental representation spontaneously produced at a deeper level in the brain.

Thinking in images requires us not just to look at an image, but also to "enter into it." Rather than naming an object (a table, a chair) then describing it intellectually (of course it has four legs), we wait for the image to "reveal itself," studying it with a curious gaze, as though looking out from a viewpoint at the landscape below cloaked in dense fog that only gradually dissipates — the image must appear "unbeknownst" and not be forced.

Thinking in images requires allowing the images to invade our mind, then slowly letting them drift together "on their own." It is not about telling a story, but about first "seeing" then "feeling" the immobile image that has taken from before our eyes.

This exercise, practiced in a group context, is an essential element of collective creativity. The shared "seeing" of an image is one of the steps in the common construction of what will become a shared nascent idea.

This revealed-image group exercise should not be confused with such neighboring techniques as the imaginative story, the fantasy story (positive or negative), or collective wakeful dreaming, all of which are techniques used at different moments for different objectives.

- In the imaginary story, a tale is constructed. For example, visiting a home, a factory, or a cave together. It could be a children's tale that respects that language (Once upon a

time... Every day... Then one day... Because of that... Up until... Ever since then...), or the building of a plot.
- Fantasy elements with a negative nuance (a nightmare) or a positive nuance (paradise) can be added. The injection of fantasy elements liberates the imagination and encourages unbridled imaginative production. But attention must be paid to not letting the tale become preposterous.
- In wakeful dreaming, we not only travel to an exterior environment, such as a landscape, a city, etc., but also travel through it. With their eyes closed, the members of the group sit or lie comfortably in a circle. The facilitator suggests an image, and each participant, as he feels inspired, imaginatively describes what he sees. First one at a time, then the group as a whole, freely imagines the image, introducing unforced fantasy elements, exploring an imaginary planet, or wakeful dreaming about various common subjects: we're going to travel in a car engine, through a house, in a watch. When generating ideas, the theme of the voyage is chosen in relation to the creative challenge in order to facilitate crossing-over. The wakeful dreaming is a key indicator of the group dynamic; it is often a test of the group cohesion.

Practical Context
- Teaching sensitive association

The "little bicycle" technique is distinct in that it teaches a basic language that encourages the subsequent production of different modalities of imaginary construction, as well as the emergence of ideas. It is a necessary point of passage in a group workshop — a group cannot function in the sensitive stance until it has succeeded in merging with the progressively revealed image.
- Creative problem-solving process

The "little bicycle" is not only a language; it is a technique that can be used in all of the stages of creative problem solving:

- In exploring the challenge: imaginative merging can be used during the exploratory phase of the problem in order to intuitively feel the problem beyond its rational formula.

- In generation of ideas: It is typically a departure technique that encourages the generation of imaginary material. This imaginary material can be produced by commenting on a drawing, describing an , recounting an imaginary tale, etc.
The emergence of ideas, as though appearing out of a fog, is by nature the language of the "little bicycle," and is the most symbolic moment of this method. For example, in the "lookout" phase, when the group is sensitively, actively listening, striving to find a connection between the imaginary material and the challenge so as to allow a fuzzy idea to emerge, or in the pendulum exercise, when the members of the group let their imagination freely float between two opposing limits.

- In the stage where the group chooses and expands on solutions: the "little bicycle" technique is a precious tool in helping enhance solutions, notably through a sensitively written exploration of the concept.

Implementation in teaching sensitive association
In this stage of the workshop, the group sits in a circle, their eyes closed. The members of the group begin to free associate with simple shapes, common practical objects.

Generally, participants are too verbal, imposing their vision of the object on the rest of the group. Each member of the group must learn to reveal only a snippet of the object so that everyone gets a chance to express himself.

Exercises implicating emotion, such as the "passing gestures," help to clarify the link between the three key stages:
   a) Listening
   b) Association
   c) Expression

The members of the group must learn to let the nascent image flood them, as opposed to describing a concept or telling a story.

Exercises relating to more complex themes can then be employed before passing to the "little bicycle" technique.
The language of the "little bicycle" then becomes a sort of code. We will often suggest: "go ahead, brainstorm," or "now let's do the 'little bicycle.'"

Implementation in the creative problem-solving process
Here it is carried out in three stages:

Departure stage: regardless of the meta-step in the creative problem-solving process, we start with the departure stage, using the "little bicycle" technique (imaginative association) described above. This departure toward the imagination and sensations helps to open up new imaginative horizons, skewed paths that invite new discoveries.
Emergence stage: here we slowly let the imaginary material intersect with reality.

Sensitive convergence stage: the nascent idea that has finally emerged is given weight, enriched, and reinforced.

Practical Guide: Identification

Objectives
To emotionally, "physically" feel the problem, to identify with an element of the problem (you become the problem: experience the grinding gears, the stretch of the nylon thread...), encourages the generation of rich, often surprising imaginative material. This is an absorbing, projective individual technique (used in group workshops), and much like dreaming.

Practical Context
It is typically a departure technique that encourages an emotional approach to the challenge, often opening up new paths; but it can also be used in the exploratory stage, to better discern the problem. The group should have previously learned the crossing-over technique and should have developed a trusting group climate.

Implementation
One member of the group sits with his eyes closed, in a state of abandonment, concentrates on feeling the targeted aspect of the chosen problem, and verbalizes what he would feel if, say, he were a coil. *"The creative technical person can think himself to be a dancing molecule, discarding the detachment of the expert and throwing himself into the activity of the elements involved. He becomes one of the molecules."* (W. J. J. Gordon)
He must cut himself off from his environment and place himself in a dream state, since identification is in fact much like dreaming. For the exercise to work, he must form a real emotional attachment to the identification. (Doing a few relaxation exercises beforehand can be helpful.)

There are two crossing-over methods: one direct, in which the deepening leads, fuzzy or fragmented ideas that appear to each in the group, are written in notebooks; and one indirect, in which we record and then listen back to the recording using the "lookout" technique (see Family 2: crossing-over techniques for the emergence of ideas).

Practical Guide: Analogy and Metaphor

Dynamic Stance: Analogy
This is what we call direct analogy, which allows for straightforward, explicit connections. Here we search out a new manner of comparison while respecting similarities of technique, practicality, and usage, which can then inspire the generation of new ideas. For example:

- To generate ideas on how to keep a floor smooth, you could take inspiration from the technique of leveling a skating rink.
- In cosmetics, you could compare the elasticity of skin with a pair of jeans made with Lycra.
- You could compare the folding mechanism of a chaise lounge with the way in which a praying mantis folds its legs.

Sensitive Stance: Metaphor
The sensitive technique draws on metaphors, parables, or poetic description. A metaphor draws on archetypal material, on symbols that speak to the collective imagination.

Objectives
Shift the essence of the creative challenge to a new paradigm or sphere in order to stimulate the mechanisms of creative resolution.

Practical Context
This is a very powerful technique for generating new leads for ideas or to illustrate solutions. Analogy helps to highlight rational belief, whereas metaphors are useful in highlighting emotional belief.

Implementation
We list the words, verbs, adjectives linked to the heart of the creative challenge and extract the essence. (This phase is often quite straightforward, especially if the group has thoroughly explored the problem beforehand using mind-mapping, or if it has already spent ample time in a divergence stage.)

Brainstorm to find analogies and metaphors in other areas. Choose an analogy or metaphor; develop the essence of the analogy or metaphor; describe it; then search for parallels, ideas that directly respond to the problem at hand.

Practical Guide: Non-Verbal Departure Techniques

The rule is to short-circuit language
Language is the noblest achievement of Homo sapiens ; it is the basis of all mental evolution. *Logos* means both language and thought, as if those two notions were fused. Language translates the slow progression of the limbic system, with its reptilian-like reflexes, to the neocortex, which plays a role in abstract thought and intelligence.

Words are the tools we use to formulate a thought and communicate it to others. Words give form and structure to indistinct images and dreams. But though they translate a vague intuition into a comprehensible social code, they imprison us in a network of ancient, well-known, recorded significations, offering us answers to repeatedly asked questions.

In order to actually create, the voyage must be taken backwards from the neocortex to the limbic brain — the reptilian brain, the child's brain — to call up associative links different from those organized and constantly repeated with social language. We must return to the pre-logic, the pre-language stage. Koestler[51] sums it up wonderfully: *"true creation begins where language leaves off."*

How to short-circuit language

To short-circuit normal social language, we use:
- Associative language, favoring "thought in pictures" (infantile, fantastical) and the illogical, irrational, subjective links between them (see the "little bicycle" section).
- Drawings, particularly non-figurative, spontaneous, as well as all manner of illustrative expression.
- Corporeal movement

1. Drawing

Objectives

Drawing is the regal technique by which to express a problem imaginatively, intuitively, unconsciously, without words. Drawings should be produced only after the group has thoroughly explored the creative challenge.

Practical Context

Drawing is stressed in the departure stage. It stimulates the imagination, which will then be engaged in the emergence

---

[51] Arthur Koestler, *op. cit.*

phase in "crossing-over" the content of the drawing with the set problem. Drawing is frequently used to exploit analogies and metaphors. As we noted earlier, the analogy mechanism is in and of itself a departure, more or less substantial. Certain analogies remain in the realm of the rational, metaphors veer towards the imagination, and thus it is often interesting to exploit them with a sensitive technique like drawing.

Implementation
When we talk about "drawing," we are really talking about expressive images, or "lines and marks traced on paper" to signify that we are simply letting ideas freely express themselves through our hands and not trying to make figurative, representative, or esthetic drawings.

The choice of materials is important for the success of this technique. It is useful to have on hand a large supply of graphic material: not two or three sharp crayons, but a case full of crayons, plus markers, gouaches, tubes of acrylics, pastels, charcoal, etc. We particularly recommend finger painting, which frees up everyone's habitual relationship to drawing. The members of the group should amuse themselves with the paint; find again playful, childlike gestures.

We also recommend a large format paper, as well as an abundant supply.

Departure
There are many possible methods:
Individual drawing: everyone draws a "fuzzy idea" related to the creative challenge.
Round Robin drawing: the paper is passed around the group and everyone either adds something to the drawing or

completes the drawing using free association (this is done non-verbally, without commentary).

Collective drawing: this can be organized in sub-groups of 4 to 5 people who, depending on the situation, first discuss the subject using the "little bicycle" language, then decide on an image, or proceed non-verbally.

The walls can also be covered with Canson paper: a few members of the group begin drawing on the paper, others join in when so inspired, adding on whatever comes to them through free association. The finished product becomes a sort of "fresco" that will serve as a projective background for the group to refer back to throughout the workshop.

Emergence

The following steps should generally be followed:

It is imperative with individual or sub-group drawing that the whole group absorbs the drawing, soak up its content. To that effect, the drawing is hung on the wall and the group is encouraged to free associate using the "little bicycle" language.

Afterwards, the facilitator reintroduces the problem, and the group, inspired by the drawing, seeks out fuzzy ideas.

2. Corporeal expression

Corporeal expression is used quite frequently in creative-thinking workshops to teach groups creative mechanisms and help them experience the creative process with other than their intellects. For example, the group free associates with the "passing gestures" or "off-balance" exercises while seeking ideas, etc.

Corporeal expression can encourage the generation of ideas for two reasons.

First, it is a useful tool for assimilating the challenge: what better way to intimately understand a problem than to express it with one's body, to mimic[52] it?

Second, it works as a departure technique, in which the group can represent a concept, a mechanism, an idea with gestures, as we often do in everyday life (a food mill, tongs...), or as the deaf do with sign language. To represent an idea too vague to be described with words through movement and gesture can stimulate the generation of collective ideas.

Practical Guide: Projective Techniques

In psychology, projection is an unconscious act in which a person "projects" his own positive and negative affects onto others; it is a defense mechanism that helps in shaping the ego. It has been used in psychology to build a vast base of personality tests designed to let a person respond to various stimuli (figurative or abstract drawings, for instance); their responses are written down and analyzed for meaning.

There are many different projective methods, including those in which the subject is asked to find a structure in an abstract drawing (the Rorschach inkblot is the most typical example); those where the subject is asked to interpret provocative pictures (TAT being the most well-known); word-association, developed by Jung, the precursor of projective tests; methods

---

[52] We do this with a method we have adapted from the "magician's box" technique, developed by René Bernèche. We call our adaptation "images catcher."

that stage a game, a psychodrama, serving as a pretext to get the subject to react, etc.

Two things come into play here: the quality of the visual aid and the method used.

Objective
Significantly accelerate departure through the use of the projective potential of the visual aid.

Practical Context
Following a free association exercise (see the "little bicycle" section) and a dynamic stage, to progressively stimulate the imagination.

Implementation
For clarity's sake, we have divided this section in two: visual aids and process.

Visual Aids
Anything can be used as a stimulant to facilitate an inspired connection. Leonardo da Vinci used water-stained walls as a source of inspiration in solving problems.

It is helpful to have a large, preferably calibrated collection of images at your disposal with which to allow the group to explore a broad array of evocative themes — there are many stock-image banks online (Getty, Corbis, Fotolia). Most facilitators have their own collections of figurative images (photos, collages, figurative drawings, playing cards from the Martine Walter, Isabelle Jacob, Piepoli series); symbolic images (archetypal, Tarot cards, images from the Euréka series, etc.), or abstract photos.

The group could also be asked to make its own projective material from different photos taken individually, collages, and drawings.

Process
The objective is to establish a link between the ideas generated with the visual aids and the challenge.

There is a difference between the forced-connection technique and the projective crossing-over technique. In the forced-connection technique an image, word, phrase, or object is introduced between the creative challenge and the person seeking new ideas. He is then urged to create a *forced* mental connection between them.

Random words, images, or objects are chosen and the person sidesteps the normal thought process by creating an artificial connection. *"You're looking for ideas in the IT field; here are some words, some images of clouds, boats, flowers. Now find an idea that connects the two."* This exercise is normally done at a rapid pace, provoking the group to dynamically brainstorm without giving them time to think.

In the projective crossing-over technique, the pace is much slower, and here we use the sensitive "little bicycle" language.
There are two approaches to the projective crossing-over technique.

A) Explore the visual aid imaginatively
In this approach the members of the group strive to connect imaginatively, emotionally, poetically with the visual aid.
A member of the group focuses on one of the available images and enters into a departure phase: he concentrates on the emotional, sensitive, poetic dimension of the image in question.

Then, in an emergence phase, he slowly connects what he has generated during the departure phase with the creative challenge, and in a sensitive convergence notes down the fragments of ideas on Post-its.

B) Project the need of finding a solution

In this approach, the group is urged to explore and assimilate the set problem, as well as the need to find a solution. The group might even be divided into two sub-groups in order to create an atmosphere of anxiety around the search for a solution. Each sub-group then strives to "project" the need onto a visual aid. Imagine Gutenberg, obsessed by the need to reproduce the Bible and to come up with a means by which to print it. He "thinks of nothing else." He is so obsessed that, one day, while out in the countryside, seeing a group of grape pickers pressing their grapes, he "projects" his problem onto them and imagines creating a press with which he can easily print his texts. This is the attitude that must be sparked in the group by asking them to "project" their need for a solution onto the projective material. For practical purposes, we call this the "hidden solution" technique.

After the group has assimilated the desire and the need to find a solution, they are shown a handful of images. They are told, *The solution to your problem is hidden in this image. Find it! Who can feel it, who can see a fragment of it?* The playful aspect of the challenge stimulates curiosity, facilitating the generation of numerous leads to ideas.

Family 2: Crossing-Over Techniques for the Emergence of Ideas

During the crossing-over stage, we often tell the group to "be on the lookout." Indeed, the group finds itself in a situation similar to that of a hunter advancing through an unknown forest and on the lookout for clues in hopes of flushing out a rare bird.
The most effective method for this attitude of being on the lookout is to consider the clues generated during the departure stage (recording) with the gaze of a hunter seeking the "traces of ideas." The group can also achieve a "crossing-over" while listening to the group member who is "thinking imaginatively" out loud.

There are different ways of accomplishing this attitude: either abruptly seizing on an idea as it bursts forth, or slowly, gradually bringing to the surface the fledgling idea, or fragments of the idea, much as a fisherman slowly reels in his catch once it bites.

Different techniques help to facilitate this crucial phase.

Three Drawings

Pendulum

Orchestra Conductor

Staircase

Island in the Fog

Practical Guidelines: "Three Drawings"

Objectives
This technique is not only a method by which to generate ideas, but also a pedagogical tool that helps the members of a group to understand the emergence mechanism and the progression through the three stages: imaginative thinking, sketching out the idea, finalizing the idea. The imagination is significantly brought into play in the first stage.

Practical Context
During a training or lengthy creative problem-solving process, to give the members of the group sufficient time to explore the three drawings.

Implementation
This technique involves three phases:

The first is carried out individually. A large piece of paper is placed in front of a member of the group who is asked to meditate on and assimilate the creative challenge. He is then asked to draw what has surfaced in his imagination in the form of a non-figurative, improvised drawing with no particular coherent meaning, translating his imaginative thoughts into blotches of color. We recommend finger painting for this exercise, which is less precise and encourages the person to "speak with his body" in a somewhat regressive behavior.

During the second phase he makes a second drawing, this time using a paintbrush, in which he "extracts" the first strong leads or fragments of ideas. The exercise becomes more formal and the other members of the group can now offer their thoughts or ideas.

In the third phase, the ideas that have surfaced during the second phase are formulated, once again in a drawing, but this time with more definition, more polish. Here other drawing tools, such as pens and markers, can be used and collage or text added. The group has now moved from the imaginative process to the actual construction of a concept. This phase can be carried out in small groups, making use of the imaginary material mined in the preceding phases.

Practical Guidelines: "Pendulum"

Objectives
Encourage the participants to become particularly attentive to the slower-paced emergence of ideas, alternating departure and emergence.

Practical Context
Either in a training where this technique acts as a necessary point of passage allowing each participant, in succession, to "physically sense" the moment of emergence; or in the phase where ideas are generated to create a break following a collective exercise and introducing an individual sequence.

Implementation
After having assimilated the creative challenge and generated imaginative content (drawings inspired by the challenge, for example), each member of the group successively sits in a chair. The facilitator then stands behind the person, places his hands on his shoulders, and starts rocking him back and forth

from left to right, symbolizing a swaying between the imagination and the problem.

As the participant rocks to one side, the coach asks him to describe his imaginative production (his drawing, for example), then slowly rocks him to the other side, inviting him to make a connection with the challenge and offer leads for possible solutions. This rocking back and forth is repeated a number of times, concentrating on one extremity or the other depending on the content.

The rest of the group, taking the stance of a "fish bowl," free-associates, stretching the proposed leads.

Practical Guidelines: "Orchestra Conductor"

This technique is related to that of the pendulum, except that here it is done collectively.

The facilitator, as the orchestra conductor, "conducts" two sub-groups of 3 to 4 people.

The first group's mission is to produce imaginative thoughts, while the second group steers those thoughts back toward the creative problem. Like a conductor conducting the violins and horns of an orchestra with his baguette, the facilitator encourages one group to express itself then brings the sound down and turns to the other group, alternating between the imaginary pole and the challenge pole, summoning up the emergence. The rest of the group free-associates, stretching the proposed leads.

Practical Guidelines: "Staircase"

Objectives
Stimulate the group to progressively transform the imaginative stimuli into ideas at first fuzzy, then gradually, increasingly more precise.

Practical Context
During a training, to encourage the group to become keenly aware of the evolution and to slow down the tendency to generate ideas prematurely.

Implementation
The group proceeds step by step, as though descending a staircase. In practice, we ask the group to install three or four paperboards. On the first board we write "beginning ideas" where the stimulus that seems the most promising and that the group has chosen based on their individual intuition is written down. On the second board we steer the proposed idea a bit toward the creative challenge, still in a vague, sketchy form: *"is there the fragment of a solution in this idea?"* Moving down a step on the third board, the group notes positive criticisms with sentences that begin with *"To make it work, we need to...."*

Each step of this exercise prompts a new search for ideas.

Practical Guidelines: "Island in the Fog"

Objectives
Encourage the group to collectively free-associate and generate ideas, and to facilitate a slow, focused production.

Practical Context

In this technique the group should be skilled in the imaginative language of the "little bicycle" so we can use it in training. We also use it at the beginning of an emergence sequence in our workshops, when the group is exploring the material generated in the departure stage for the first time. It is very useful while generating ideas and also encourages the group's cohesion, helping to identify its weaknesses.

Implementation

To begin with, we ask the group to imagine an island in the middle of nowhere but on which the solution can be found. The island is cloaked in fog. As the fog slowly dissipates, the solutions begin to emerge. *"Slowly discover them. Who sees a vague shape?"*

This technique can be used only following a strong assimilation phase.

Family 3: Sensitive Convergence Techniques for the Elaboration of Ideas

The "sensitive" convergence stage is in effect not so different from that of the "dynamic" convergence stage. However, the specific natures of the ideas that emerge in the sensitive stance often require a slower, more meticulous approach. A slow convergence is required so as not disturb the subtle, imaginary charge that might be hiding behind the nascent idea.

Hits and highlights "On the Fly"

Intuitive clusters

Sensitive development of clusters

Concept Box©

Practical Guidelines: "Hits & Highlights" - a dynamic convergence technique

In order to better understand the different approaches between sensitive convergence and dynamic convergence techniques, we would like to remind you of the functioning principle of an emblematic convergence technique in the dynamic stance.

Objectives
Highlight the main themes of the divergence stage in order to facilitate rephrasing and turning them into solutions. When we generate a quantity of ideas and note them on Post-its, we then have to "creatively sort" them in order to arrive at a synthesis and to proceed in regrouping them by families or fragments of ideas.

Practical Context
During a creative-thinking workshop in which numerous Post-its have been produced in the divergence stage.

Implementation
This technique involves three stages:

- Search for "hits."
- Assemble everything that has previously been produced, making sure that everyone in the group has read over each idea noted on the Post-its.
- Place colored adhesive labels above the ideas, using different colored labels to classify the "hits" in relation to the specific criteria of the challenge.

Examples for different colored labels:
- Green for ideas that are felt to correspond to the creative challenge or that seem workable.

- Purple for ideas that are stimulating, but which are still vague, either in terms of feasibility or relevance to the challenge.
- Red for ideas that are considered unrealistic due to legal issues, existing patents.

Clustering: thematic grouping
In this second phase, the ideas are thematically organized into groupings, or clusters of ideas, classing each "hit" by theme or category.

First, give a title (containing at least two words) for each cluster, then place each Post-it (unlabeled) under the corresponding cluster. This can be done quite rapidly as a group.

Reformulate
This step is significant in that reformulating should express the essence of various ideas on Post-its.

Go back over each cluster and share the various potential ideas or fragments of ideas that seem to emerge from each theme.
Identify any possible common themes and then regroup or refine if necessary.

Now, using the content of the themes, ask open-ended questions in order to determine how well the themes respond to the original objective ("*How can we*" ... "*What would happen if*" ... "*How could we begin*"...), without any specific value judgment. This reformulation will be either comprised of a heading, the various Post-its, and an actual descriptive phrase, or developed in a concept board.

Practical Guidelines: Hits and highlights called "On the Fly"

Objectives
A variation on the "hits and highlights" technique, adapted here to the sensitive stance, which is useful in transforming the nascent idea into one that is more detailed, or even the beginning of a solution.

Practical Context
Contrary to the dynamic hits and highlights approach described above, here ideas are grouped and developed immediately during the ideas generation step.

Implementation
Each time a vague idea or "hit" is thought to be interesting, it is developed. We are trying to capture the spark of a nascent idea and flesh it out with the group.

In the emergence stage, the moment the facilitator or a member of the group senses a hit, the rest of the group is asked to class the Post-its associated with that hit and possibly generate new ideas.

The facilitator then asks the group to free-associate using the "little bicycle" language, summoning the nascent idea to the surface, after which it becomes possible to expand on it. This approach assists in finalizing idea sheets or solution sheets from throughout the workshop.

Practical Guidelines: intuitive clusters

Objective
A second variation on the "hits and highlights" technique adapted for the sensitive stance.

Practical Context
After an idea-generating stage in which numerous Post-its have been produced.

Implementation
At the end of an idea-generating stage, after the group has produced a wall full of Post-its, the facilitator asks everyone to intuitively make connections between the Post-its (by mental association, finding links between them but without reorganizing them). Each member of the group, individually and silently, writes down the tips of solutions he sees emerging, "sensitively harvesting" the field of ideas. Each in the group lets his or her gaze wander across the numerous Post-its, allowing solutions to surface.

This individual exercise encourages the members of the group to identify more strongly with the possible solutions. It requires a certain flexibility to keep from analytically grouping ideas and to accept "giving free rein" to their thoughts. Levi-Strauss spoke of the importance of "giving free rein," an equestrian expression that stands for letting the horse be the guide.

Practical Guidelines: sensitive development of clusters

Objectives
Emotionally and imaginatively reload the description of an idea to keep from prematurely writing it down or giving it too much rational meaning.

Practical Context
This technique is practiced after the "hits and highlights" technique (the dynamic approach).

Implementation
This technique is used in a sensitive convergence phase, to stretch the various themes, giving them more body and weight through rational and, more importantly, imaginative and emotional descriptions.

Groups of 3 to 4 free-associate using the "little bicycle" language, without Post-its, to enrich a cluster of Post-its. The facilitator records what the group "sees" rather than understands, inviting them to use metaphors, analogies, even visual aids, to express their common vision of the cluster.

The group could also develop the themes by writing solution sheets or concept boards.

Practical Guidelines: "Concept Box©"

Objective
Associate the emotional and rational aspects of the concept and give more coherence to the innovation process.

The Concept Box© helps to conserve and enrich the creative material, the "hit" having initiated the birth of a concept. The enriched concept activates mental imagery and its associated sensitive dimension.

Practical Context
The Concept Box© is a complementary technique used with in-house teams to insure the valid, coherent development of a concept and to facilitate its communication.

This approach is often indispensible when different creative profiles (marketers, designers, photographers, editors) get together. It is useful following a thematic grouping (cf. "hits and highlights" guidelines) for expanding on the theme.

Implementation
Gather together all of the generated content (conceptual, written, visual, video, textual, olfactive, sensory) in order to view it as a whole and to better understand, see, perceive, and sense a concept. For this exercise it is useful to use:
- Mind mapping
- Organized lists of key data from the project
- Metaphors and analogies
- Key points of studies (real or reconstructed verbatims from qualitative studies, ethnography, ethnological videos, documentary studies, benchmarks, competitive intelligence).

Bibliography

A list of French reference books on creative thinking, some of which inspired us in the writing of this text... among a very large number of English books about creativity!

Books on creative-thinking techniques and methods

Guy Aznar, *Idées*, Editions d'Organisation, 2005
Pierre Berloquin, *La recherche d'idées,* Bayard, 1993
Luc de Brabandère, *Le latéroscope,* La renaissance du livre, 1989
Luc de Brabandère, *Le Management des Idées*, Dunod, 1998
Luc de Brabandère, *Le plaisir des Idées*, Dunod, 1994
Patrick Duhoux, Isabelle Jacob, *Développer sa créativité*, Retz, 2006
Michel and Bernadette Fustier, *Exercices pratiques de créativité*, Editions d'organisation, 2001
Hubert Jaoui, *La créativité mode d'emploi*, ESF, 1996
Florence Vidal, *L'instant créatif*, Flammarion, 1984.
Jean-Claude Widouw, *Créativité mode d'emploi,* Editions d'Organisation, 1997
Olwen Wolfe, *J'innove comme on respire*, Editions du Pallio, 2008

Books on innovation management

Marjolaine de Ramecourt, François-Marie Pons, *L'innovation à tous les étages,* Editions d'organisation, 2001
Paul-Hubert des Mesnards, Michel Sallé, *Le management par la vision*, Editions Creargie, 2000
Isaac Getz, Alan G.Robinson, *Vos idées changent tout,* Editions d'organisation, 2003

Nathalie Joulin, *Les coulisses des nouveaux produits,* Édition d'Organisation, 2002
Abraham Moles and Roland Caude, *Créativité et méthodes d'innovation,* Fayard, 1970.

Books on creative function and functioning of the brain

Henri Atlan, *Création et créativité,* Editions Castella, 1961
Gaston Bachelard, *Le droit de rêver,* PUF, 1970
René Boirel, *L'invention,* PUF, 1966
Jean-Pierre Changeux and Alain Cones, *Matière à pensée,* Odile Jacob, 1989
Robert Desoille, *Le rêve éveillé en psychothérapie,* PUF, 1945
Carla Hannaford, *La gymnastique des neurones,* Editions Jacques Grancher, 1997
Todd Lubart, *Psychologie de la créativité,* Armand Colin, 2003
Paul Mac Lean, Roland Guyot, *Les trois cerveaux de l'homme,* Robert Laffont, 1990
Edgar Morin, *Introduction à la pensée complexe,* ESF, 1990

THE SENSITIVE STANCE IN THE PRODUCTION OF CREATIVE IDEAS

www.ingramcontent.com/pod-product-compliance
Lightning Source LLC
Chambersburg PA
CBHW061448040426
42450CB00007B/1271